I AM AN ECHO CHAMBER
THE BASIS OF TRIBALISM

Other works by this author:

You're Not Nuts... You've Just Got Issues. Outskirts
Press, Parker, CO, 2006.

For Parents & Teens: A Guide To Peaceful Coexistence.
Outskirts Press, Parker, CO, 2007.

Them There Guys: An Epistolary Odyssey. With David
B. Finkelstein. Lulu Press, 2010.

Selfonomics: How Broadly-defined Self-Interest Ex
plains Everything!. ttgPress, 2014.

Essays. With David B. Finkelstein. ttgPress, 2015.

The Legacy Book: A Guided (Auto)biography. 2017,
ttgPress.

When Technology And Self-Interest Collide: (Watch
Out!). ttgPress, 2017.

Them There Eyes: And The Woman Behind Them.
ttgPress, 2017.

I AM AN ECHO CHAMBER

THE BASIS OF TRIBALISM

Anthony J. Gribin

ttgPress 2018

First Printing: 2018

ISBN 978-0-9993006—2-6

ttgPress

19 Make Dr.
Wayside, N.J. 07712

ajgribin@optonline.net

Dedication

To those whose echo chambers revere logic, respect science and seek truth.

Contents

Acknowledge*me*

It all started around 1990, when a friend of mine named Matt Schiff and I decided to write an intellectual tome on the subject of doo-wop music. There was virtually nothing written about it, which left the field wide open for two aspiring "Doctors of Doo-Wop." Our short-lived fame led to appearances on radio and cable TV, writing liner notes for three CDs and being minor celebrities among the generation of people who love that kind of music for at least five minutes.

The biggest takeaway for me from that experience was that I enjoyed writing. A lot. I've written a few pop psychology books based on my career as a psychologist. I write with humor (if I do say so myself) and use math to illustrate points that I'm trying to make to the reader. I've transcribed and annotated journals from my college years and written a humorous memoir (humoir? dicklit?) with a friend from childhood, Dave Finkelstein.

I flit from subject to subject, as the reader might have noticed. I put out a book to allow people to, in effect, write the story of their lives ("The Legacy Book: a guided (auto)biography") which led me to write a biography of my mother, Doris Tauber, who was a well-known composer of popular music.

Over the last few years I've written three books that involve a theory that I've called "Selfonomics," which speaks to the overlap between psychology and behavioral economics. "Selfonomics" was the first effort; "When Self-Interest and Technology Collide" was the second; this book being the third.

If it seems as if I'm bragging, let me take myself down a few pegs: none of these books sell more than a handful of copies, with the exception of those on doo-wop music. They are a product of "publishing on demand," or P.O.D., so there is no cost to me as the author, and very little danger that anything I pen will besmirch the best seller list. So why do I bother?

Because it's fun. As I've gotten older and developed orthopedic issues, I've had to curtail almost all but sedentary activity. So I write about things that interest me, which has both good and bad consequences. The good part is that since I'm interested in any subject that I, for whatever strange reason, choose to focus on, it's not a chore. I look forward to stolen moments alone with my computer. The bad part is that since I've arrived late to the game for any subject that I've chosen, I feel, and perhaps write, like the "new guy on the block." I have no (for want of a better phrase) "book cred."

My career as a psychologist has been spent doing psychotherapy. I'm not attached to a university and haven't done *real* research since graduate school. I have no peers from whom to get input and criticism for what I've written in my field. My theorizing, as my dear wife Gloria is quick to point out, is just that, and might be considered merely very long Op-Ed columns. And though I've given some of the manuscripts to bright friends from whom I hoped for comments, the modal response is silence. I can picture them leafing through the pages, losing interest quickly, and then trying to avoid the subject when they see me. They kid me about my hobby, saying something like "Gribin's probably finishing up his second volume on [fill in the blank subject]," after the first time it comes up in conversation.

In turn, I kid a friend, Joe Landau, who has a successful bookbinding business in New York, and knows all aspects of the publishing field, about when he's going to get me published by a legitimate book concern. He has made some sincere efforts, but I know the bar to entry for that kind of thing is pretty high. And since I don't have a "name" in any given field, meaning I don't have a natural audience for what I've written, Joe's come up empty. I do appreciate his efforts, however. (Joe... it's time to step up your game!)

I continue to write because I can, because I get to dwell on subjects that interest me, and because it allows me to still feel vital despite my years. In effect, writing is an act of liberating myself from the boredom that I associate with advancing age. It allows me to feel proud of *me*. And that's why this section is spelled the way it is.

Preface

This book has a very simple message: *Confirmation bias, guided by deductive and inductive logic, driven by self-interest, catalyzed by technology, all within a person's unique echo chamber, leads to tribalism.* Okay, maybe it's not that simple.

This is not another book on Donald Trump, but his election to the Presidency in 2016 sped up changes to our society that were looming for decades. His name, therefore, will be mentioned frequently.[1] He is sure to be pleased.

Dissatisfaction with Bill Clinton's "escapades" helped George W. Bush beat Al Gore in electoral votes, despite losing the popular vote. Bush's bellicosity led to the election of Barack Obama, who was seen as someone who would get us out of distant wars. Obama's belief in diversity, globalization and inclusion aided Donald Trump in besting Hilary Clinton, who was seen as an extension of her former boss.

Donald Trump's first year in office has, with or without intention, exposed fault lines in American society. He didn't do it alone. The march towards globalization, illegal immigration and growing income inequality hasn't helped. Galloping technology with

---

[1] One hundred and twenty-nine times, excluding footnotes and references.

the resultant outsourcing, mechanization and elimination of jobs and whole industries has adversely affected many of our citizens.

The effect of the Trump presidency has been to "take the gloves off." "No holds barred…" Lying, exaggerating, distracting or deflecting has become almost universal in political messaging. Trump verbally rips into such institutions as the Courts, our intelligence services, the media and Congress. He uses Twitter to circumvent mainstream media and talk directly to his base. While bias has always been present (for one cannot be totally objective), it is now open and obvious in almost every news story and political issue. Trump has laughed at political correctness, taken the defense mechanism of projection to new heights and abandoned civility. His behavior, as well as his words, have said, "You're either for me or against me. Choose!" And the people who have chosen to be in the against column, fearing a march to autocracy, have gotten increasingly fearful, enraged and engaged. This is the country that America has become as of the beginning of 2018.

But back to the message of this book. Almost all of the terms in the first paragraph… confirmation bias, deductive and inductive logic, self-interest and unique echo chambers are found *within each person and are interdependent and interrelated*. Technology is outside of us, and tribalism is the observed effect on society. What this implies is that both the source of the increase in tribalism as well as the remedy for that increase, if one is desired, lies within each of us. As will become clear, these internal processes are not pathological or wrong; they are natural, genetic and eminently human.

Introduction

"There might be conservatives or liberals, but people generally could agree on a baseline of reality. One of the dangers of the internet is that people can have entirely different realities. They can just be cocooned in information that reinforces their current biases."

-President Barack Obama, in a BBC interview conducted by Prince Harry of England, broadcast on December 27, 2017.

Let's go back a few years… Our ancestors lived in tribes. If another tribe, hostile to the first, attacked or threatened to attack, desirous of food, weapons or women, the first tribe would experience fear, anger or some combination of the two. They would then take appropriate action: fight or flee. If they just sat there, they would be conquered and die. If they fought or fled, they had a shot.

The better fighters and flee-ers survived to pass on their DNA. Turning the other cheek didn't cut it. A better maxim was "an eye for an eye." The fight or flight responses are protective self-interest, honed into us through the millennia; etched into us through evolution. We've only become civilized in the last (being generous) few thousand years.

These days, attacks still come in the form of physical assault or its threat. Witness the "Troubles" of Northern Ireland, the Balkan Wars of the 1990s, and much of what obtains in the Middle East to this day (Syria, Iraq, Yemen, Israel-Palestine, ISIS-everyone else).

Physical attacks have happened in this country as well. The Indian Wars, protests in the cities in the 1960s and most notably, our Civil War. More common, however, at least in the middle of the second decade of the twenty-first century, are verbal attacks. Which brings us to Donald Trump…who has made household names of the terms confirmation bias, echo chambers, fake news, white supremacy, tribalism, and other fun words and phrases.

The tribalism brought on by Trumpism was not only of Trump's doing. The people that voted for him did so for a variety of reasons. He is entertaining, which contrasts with the meaningless platitudes proffered by most other politicians. He doesn't speak the King's English; his vocabulary, spelling and grammar allow a connection to people who felt left out of the
political process. He is anti-intellectual, unlike his predecessor, Barack Obama. George W. Bush was elected in part as a reaction to Bill Clinton. Obama

was elected as a reaction to Bush, and Trump was elected as a response to the eight years of Obama.

Hillary Clinton was not a great candidate, although that's easy to say in hindsight. Her mishandling of emails and the Benghazi investigation, though nothing-burgers, allowed FBI Director Jim Comey to trip over his own feet and throw a monkey wrench into the campaign. The alt-right and the Russians pushed fake stories and the Trump campaign jumped on them and magnified them. This may have been a game of footsie between the Russians and people in Trump's circle, or it could have been opportunistic. Not that it matters much to the outcome of the election; it worked. And Trump's constant lying, name-calling and finger pointing weren't countered by any effective strategy, either by Democrats or Republicans who vowed, for a New York minute, "never Trump."

There were also trends in society, some direct and some indirect, that were involved in his victory. Income inequality, racial tensions, global competition, unemployment, automation, the power of technology and the complexity of information all led to a large plurality of voters falling on their swords for Trump.

These topics will be discussed in detail in later chapters. But despite losing the popular vote, 45.9% to Clinton's 48.0% (getting almost 3 million less votes than Clinton), he still won the electoral college.

Another set of reasons for increasing tribalism concerns our Constitution and the idiosyncratic characteristics of American society. The Second Amendment divides us into pro- and anti-gun groups. The rules governing the relationships between races divided us so starkly that it led to our Civil War. The Electoral College has given us Presidents who have lost the popular vote twice in this century alone (George W. Bush and Donald J. Trump). The method of assigning Senators and Representatives gives more weight to rural, less populous states than urban, more populated ones. Gerrymandering allows distortion of proportionate voting, as does the tendency of liberals to cluster in big cities. And our system of capitalism, which we hold in such high esteem, tilts the economic playing field to favor the wealthy.

There's a third set of causes of tribalism...we the people. There are things about the way we are put together psychologically that leads us to look out for ourselves, sometimes at the expense of others. Even though we no longer are in a world where it's kill or be killed, as obtained thousands of years ago, we still possess qualities that were honed by evolution which allow modern tribal animosities and fears. If a person is attacked verbally, they will react the same way an ancient ancestor did; they will "fight or flee." If the person attacking them has power, think of a boss or the police or a President, they may "flee." Thus a secretary may abide a boss's sexual advances, an immigrant may hide from ICE (Immigration and Customs Enforcement) or many people may fear losing health coverage. If the aggressor has less power, or is perceived to be illegitimate, they may fight back with words, reacting with hatred or fear or both, but it is clear that animosity will be directed at the person or groups doing the attacking. Divisiveness results and there will be no warm cuddlies.

This book will delve into what goes on within us individually and as a species that allows and supports the increase in tribalism. What we will find is that we are all subject to confirmation bias, to living in echo chambers, to thinking logically and following our self-interest. And while these are all human attributes, in combination with the amount and spread of information, they make the world a more difficult and even dangerous place to live in.

Chapter 1: The Echo Chamber

How can it be that both staunch Conservatives and dyed-in-the-wool Liberals are so sure their beliefs are *the* correct ones? How can it be that a member of a particular religion believes that he (or she) has *the* right answer? Or even how I can walk out of a movie theater or restaurant thinking that what I saw or ate was the cat's meow, while my wife thinks the movie was boring or the food stunk?

The phrase, "That's what makes horse racing" comes to mind. This phrase, which is usually meant as an off the cuff remark to explain why I ordered chicken and you ordered steak, will prove to have an important role in the way humans think. "Don't be put off by colleagues who are interested in different hobbies than you. There are thousands of hobbies and three hundred million people in the United States. By definition, not everyone can share the same interests! That's what makes horse racing. And basket weaving. And fencing. And - well, you get the basic idea."[2] Though seemingly trivial, whether we know it or not, this old saw has profound meaning and occupies a central place in all of our lives.

The term "echo chamber" was first used in 1937 to describe, "a room with sound-reflecting walls used

---

[2] Oliver, Vicki. <u>301 Smart Answers to Tough Business Etiquette Questions.</u> 2015, Skyhorse Publishing Co.

for producing hollow or echoing sound effects."[3] Eighty years later, in 2017, the phrase has become the property of social science and the news media and, within those, politics. To a political junkie, watching network news is not optional. In the United States, there are three major news networks: MSNBC, which by reputation tends to provide the most liberal opinions and emphases, CNN, which also leans to the left of center, and FOX, which is clearly conservative in its views. They each have their reputations, but first hand differentiation is only available to those who tune in to more than one network. If a viewer were to stick to only *one* network, they might easily assume that what they were hearing was the absolute truth.

There are two ways to measure where a network lies on the liberal-to-conservative spectrum. One involves the amount of time devoted to a particular issue and the second is the way an issue is presented. Time allotment is more objective and easier to measure. In the beginning of November 2017, men central to Trump's Presidential campaign, Paul Manafort and Rick Gates, were indicted by special counsel Robert Mueller as part of his investigation of Russian med-

dling into the 2016 Presidential campaign. This news was clearly anti-Trump and one would expect that the

---

[3] Merriam-Webster.

coverage would be more complete in left-leaning media.

Expectations were borne out. The indictments hit the airwaves at around 8:00 a.m. In the first two hours thereafter, MSNBC covered the story for 105 of the next 120 minutes, CNN 101 of 120 and FOX 54 of 120. As judged by the coverage of this story, MSNBC and CNN are more or less on the same page, and FOX is on quite another.[4]

As for the emphasis given to a particular story, that can vary widely as well. In June of 2016, Karen Tumulty, a reporter for the Washington Post, compared the way the Washington Post and the New York Times covered the Benghazi probe. The Times featured a headline, "Benghazi Panel Find No Misdeeds by Clinton" while the WAPO reported "Republicans on Benghazi panel rip U.S. response."[5]

For the adventurous souls with the good sense, energy or guts to channel surf, the distinctly differing opinions and information offered on each network can be classified as an "echo chamber," defined as "a situation in which information, ideas, or beliefs are amplified or reinforced by transmission and repetition

---

[4] Adams, Taylor, Ma, Jessica & Thompson, Stuart A. "Trump Loves 'Fox & Friends.' Here's Why." New York Times, Opinion, 11/1/17.

[5] Tumulty, Karen. "Two newspapers; two Benghazi headlines." Twitter Post, 6/29/16. See also Schumaker, Erin. "How Republicans And Democrats Can Interpret Events SO Differently." Huffpost, updated 7/1/16.

inside an 'enclosed' system, where different or competing views are censored, disallowed or otherwise underrepresented."[6] The phrase has been applied both to networks and the summation of the news they choose to broadcast.

There are other terms that describe these phenomena, the most common among them being "confirmation bias," or "the tendency to search for, interpret, favor, and recall information in a way that confirms one's beliefs or hypotheses, while giving disproportionately less consideration to alternative possibilities."[7] It seems as if what takes place *within a person* watching news within a given echo chamber *is* confirmation bias.

Confirmation bias within echo chambers is the first step toward "tribalism," defined by Merriam-Webster as "tribal consciousness and loyalty; *especially*: exaltation of the tribe above other groups."

The culture that exists at each television network is simply that it broadcasts *predominantly* information that agrees with its "slant," and avoids or dismisses information that runs counter to that slant. Attempting to portray itself as, to use an old FOX term, "fair and balanced," each network hires a representative or two from the opposing side, who is

---

[6] Source: wikipedia

[7] ibid. Other terms are selective exposure theory and false consensus effect.

basically a straw man to whom they give little more than lip service. In a way, these token pariahs help to inoculate viewers to arguments from the "bad" side, making it easier to maintain their original positions.

As a result we, the viewers, take in what we know through "network colored glasses." If we lean left, we hear news and opinions that favor the left and disparage the right, and vice versa if we lean right. With repetition, the opinions and beliefs of the viewer become more and more hardened as time goes on, forming a buffer bolstered every day by further confirmatory and supportive information.

The same situation obtains within social media. Facebook users post, click "like" and add to political arguments that they agree with. Since their Facebook "friends" are likely to agree with them, those arguments go round and round. Algorithms developed by Facebook and others ensure that people are fed information that is consistent with their views, in the same way that Walmart shoppers will get e-mails about sales at Walmart and not be informed of sales at Neiman-Marcus.

Opinions from one side rarely reach people who disagree but if they do, a person may "de-friend" (or block) the person espousing contrary opinions. Within a group of Facebook friends, the circulation of stories is akin to the "telephone game," wherein a story is passed from person to person, changing slightly each time it is passed. By the time the story has made the rounds, it has changed and likely been exaggerated. An example of this is that when Obama's birthplace was questioned when he first ran for president (the "birther movement"), the echo chamber eventually had him being a Muslim, fomenting terrorism and nattily dressed up in native African robes. Since there never was any information supporting this conspiracy theory, and there was evidence, in the form of his actual birth certificate, supporting his American heritage, it is miraculous that so many people could hang onto the belief that he was foreign-born for so long. Some still believe it! We have the echo chambers of certain news outlets and social media to thank for that.

Sometimes the information circulating within an echo chamber seems trivial or silly, but writ large, this echoic process carries a risk for the stability of our system of government because it pits some Americans against other Americans. "Confirmation bias is deepening political polarization, which is already at record levels. Our political culture is sick and getting sicker, and confirmation bias is now a leading toxin."[8]

"Tribalism only destabilizes a democracy
when it calcifies into something bigger and
more intense than our smaller, multiple

---

[8] Wehner, Peter. "Seeing Trump Through a Glass, Darkly." New York Times Op-Ed, 10/7/17.

loyalties; when it rivals our attachment to the nation as a whole; and when it turns rival tribes into enemies. And the most significant fact about American tribalism today is that all three of these characteristics now apply to our political parties, corrupting and even threatening our system of government."[9]

When the NRA calls Democrats "socialists," and Democrats see the gun lobby as the product of white nationalism, there's trouble in River City.

---

[9] Sullivan, Andrew. "America Wasn't Built for Humans." New York Magazine, 9/19/17.

Chapter 2: I Am An Echo Chamber

Thus far, the echo chamber has been discussed as a property of both news and social media. Let's now throw human beings into the mix. If I watch MSNBC (or FOX) exclusively, I become part of that system. I am exposed to left- or right-biased information that becomes part of *my own* belief system. In turn I repeat what I've heard to people with whom I interact. I espouse arguments favorable to one side, even though I don't see it as a "side," and ignore or disparage contrary information. So now, *I am part of the echo chamber*.

It is significant that I don't see my set of beliefs as a "side." I see it as the truth, and I often can't understand why others don't agree with me. The facts are plain, aren't they? How can others not see the forest for the trees? "What's easy to see in others is hard to see in ourselves. I can assure myself that my intellectual integrity is superior to theirs, yet in my honest moments I recognize that I struggle with these same human frailties and flaws."[10]

Notice what happens. I *passively filter* incoming information that is right before my eyes, on TV or Facebook or in a newspaper, to see if it is consistent with my views, but I also *actively seek out* information that is consistent with my belief system. If I lean left

---

[10] Wehner, Peter, op cit.

and hear a left-leaning conversation at the next table, I might want to join in. If the conversation is right-leaning I will avoid it (or it may even anger me). I might buy the New York Times and avoid the Wall Street Journal. *I both passively filter and actively seek confirmation of what I believe. But echo chambers in the service of politics may just be the tip of the iceberg and provide an instructive example of how we humans function in general.*

Looking further into the human condition… In general, how often do we change our minds about… anything? Most of us have a style of dressing, opinions about people and groups, religious and political beliefs, favorite sports teams, music, movies and foods. Can we change? Yes, but change is the exception, not the rule. It is slow and very difficult to obtain, even for simple things. We prefer the same flavor of ice cream, the same types of movies, the same television shows, the same styles of dress. It takes a lot to get us to change our minds. There's a lot of inertia out there, folks!

Some of these opinions are so etched into our belief systems that we can react emotionally. If my favorite team loses, especially to their rivals, I feel bad. When they win, I'm euphoric. I get angry if anyone criticizes my family member, and feel happy if friends recognize my birthday.

It seems, on closer examination, that each of us, meaning you, me and the next guy are, in effect, our own unique echo chambers. That is, whatever beliefs we hold lead us to "search for, interpret, favor, and recall information in a way that confirms [our] beliefs or hypotheses, while giving disproportionately less consideration to alternative possibilities."[11]

How could each of us *not* be a unique echo chamber? If we weren't we would often (or perhaps always) be adrift in the world of ideas, shifting our views every other minute, subject eternally to competing information, and being lost in indecision. Every choice point would require a new thought process. Thinking and deciding is hard! Sticking to our guns is easy. *It must be this way since we can't change opinions all the time and retain our identity or sanity.*

Being our own unique echo chamber means that each of us has within us a nexus, or an interlocking system of beliefs, concepts, premises, values and attitudes which are relatively fixed. We are resistant to taking in new information that does not agree with the beliefs we hold, and we *actively seek* out information that is consistent with those beliefs. This nexus of beliefs, this echo chamber, is what others may refer to as "personality." While using the word "personality" is descriptive, using the phrase "echo chamber" implies the processes that underly that personality.

---

[11] wikipedia.

Echo chambers (and/or personalities) are formed in childhood. When young our parents teach us what to believe and we, as "blank slates," absorb those ideas and keep them as our own. We can know nothing different.[12] In reverence of them, and/or occasionally in fear of them, we don't question much. We believe in Santa Claus and the Easter Bunny. We believe we will grow up to be strong if we eat certain foods, that we will get sick if we aren't dressed warmly when we go out or, perhaps, that God will punish us if we don't say our prayers. We learn to like sports, or dance or music, we root for the Raiders, or Yankees, we identify as a jock or nerd or preppy or gearhead. These notions may change as we grow older, but not easily. As we mature, our primary source of information shifts to friends and peer groups, and to our own experiences. We learn and we form that nexus of constructs that make up our individual echo chambers.

Does the rigidity of the beliefs in my echo chamber matter to anyone or any thing? Depends. If I am unbending in my love for chocolate ice cream, it doesn't affect anyone but me. If I have a strong preference for eating at Italian restaurants, the only people that might suffer are family members. In this

---

[12] This begs the question (for another time), of what happens to young children who live in a series of foster homes in their formative years, where the rules and beliefs they are taught vary from home to home.

case, there are ways to negotiate a reasonable solution, such as taking turns. But if I become intractable in my beliefs about race, religion or politics, it is likely that those will clash with the beliefs of others. Anything that promotes rigidity of beliefs in these arenas, is likely to increase tribalism. Further, since these fields are likely to have an emotional connection for us, the beliefs in this area may be not only rigid, but intensely so.

Chapter 3: Characteristics of Echo Chambers

Although each of our echo chambers is unique, they do share some common parameters that guide their contents. Among them are the length of time that a belief has been held, the emotional valence of that belief and the how the belief relates to our self-image.

The nexus of beliefs that comprise each echo chamber is likely to be *buffered*, in the sense that the longer one holds a given belief, the less it is open to change, other things being equal.[13] If we are one of three children in a family, and at the age of seven see our oldest sister as bossy, it is likely that when we become adults, she will still be seen the same way. As an adult, however, we have the choice of dealing with her imperious ways regularly, limiting the contacts to holidays (and rolling our eyes when she tells us what to do), or avoiding her entirely. The belief about Sis hasn't changed much, but our ability to deal with her has. When young, our beliefs are malleable. As we get older they become more fixed. There is evidence that neuroplasticity decreases as we age and, as they say, "You can't teach an old dog new tricks."

We can imagine ourselves as a piece of clay that hardens over time. Over the years, the clay becomes impervious to being molded (to mix metaphors) by new information. And of course, some people will be,

---

13 Freudian and Piagetian stages, at which children can be "stuck" fits here.

either temperamentally or through social learning or both, more open to new things than others. If we like to think of ourselves as "flexible," read "not rigid," we may actively seek to try new things within certain spheres, such as food, movies and activities. Flexibility may be normally distributed, though experience tells me that there may be more people on the rigid end of the scale and that rigidity will generally increase with age for all of us.

The *emotional valence* of any topic will also affect the fixedness of our beliefs. Politics, religion and race are likely to engender strong feelings in us, and our echo chambers will likely reject any contrary views. Topics less close to our hearts, such as likes and dislikes or preferences (choice of restaurant or clothing), are likely to be less incendiary and more negotiable. The less familiar I am with a particular topic and the less "skin" I have in the game, the more my beliefs may be open to change.

People can disagree and get along with each other as long as the level of emotion is relatively low. But what happens when the intensity of any issue is turned way up, as has been the case in the Trump era? When you think or know that someone doesn't like you, perhaps *hates* you, your response is equal and opposite. You dislike/hate him/her/them. As Trump has said horrible things about minorities, immigrants, intellectuals, liberals, Clinton supporters and even the Republicans he ran against in the primaries, the people and groups attacked have not been overly pleased with him. "Most Americans now feel their own group faces discrimination, according to an NPR Poll. A majority of whites say that discrimination exists against whites, even though a majority have not personally experienced it."[14]

An excellent article in Politico by Joshua Zeitz points to an emotionally-laden issue that lies deep within the echo chambers of many caucasians. Namely, that there are psychological as well as monetary advantages to being white, which can be traced back to the Reconstruction Era after the Civil War and the writings of W.E.B. Du Bois.[15] Being white allowed one admission to any public function, to the better schools and to police jobs and the appearance of equality to those wealthier than you. Blacks on the other hand were subjected to ridicule, exclusion and stricter law enforcement. One might be poor, but being white was an important and motivating consolation. In fact, this value was (and perhaps still is) so important that whites will vote against their self-interest, on issues such as siding with Republicans in opposing the ACA and tolerating tax reform that will

---

[14] Egan, Timothy. "The National Crackup." New York Times Op-Ed, 10/27/17.

[15] Zeitz, Joshua. "Does the White Working Class Really Vote Against Its Own Interests?" Politico, 12/31/17. At: https://www.politico.com/magazine/story/2017/12/31/trump-white-working-class-history-216200?cid=apn

eventually disadvantage them. It's ironic that black and white working classes *did not* band together to form a very powerful economic lobby.

In a way, this bigotry grew out of collusion between the poor whites who were allowed to feel privileged because of the color of their skin, and the upper class whites that they voted for time and time again. And yet, to this day, almost no white person will admit to being prejudiced or bigoted toward minorities. Instead they will invoke generalized rationalizations that involve laziness or immorality or criminal behavior.

With the emotional volume turned up, the result is a retreat into tribalism, where the only people you trust are "your kind," and the others are, well, "the other." That was the aim of ads paid for by Russia which injected divisive rhetoric into the 2016 Presidential campaign. Examples are a fake ad trumpeting "Muslims for Clinton," which was sure to energize the right (against the left), or "Remove Clinton from the ballot," likely to anger the left (against the right). So the meddling that the Russians did during the election period was designed to drive wedges between "us" and "them," and thus weaken our system of government.[16]

Tribalism in the extreme can be pretty scary. It describes what obtains in Syria, Iraq and Yemen in the early years of the 21st century, the conflagration in Northern Ireland in the late 20th century, as well as the war in the Balkans in the 1990s. But lately tribalism has hit much closer to home.

> "two tribes whose mutual incomprehension and loathing can drown out their love of country, each of whom scans current events almost entirely to see if they advance not so much their country's interests but their own. I mean two tribes where one contains most racial minorities and the other is disproportionately white; where one tribe lives on the coasts and in the cities and the other is scattered across a rural and exurban expanse; where one tribe holds on to traditional faith and the other is

---

[16] "A Facebook white paper in April outlined some of the methods organizations have used to create "false amplification" of content. This includes coordinated campaigns of likes, shares and comments from fake accounts, such as those set up by Russian-controlled organizations. These campaigns were conducted both on Russian-created posts and legitimate posts by news outlets and public figures." From Shapiro, Leslie. "Anatomy of a Russian Facebook ad." Washington Post, Business Analysis, 11/1/17.

increasingly contemptuous of religion altogether; where one is viscerally nationalist and the other's outlook is increasingly global; where each dominates a major political party; and, most dangerously, where both are growing in intensity as they move further apart.

The project of American democracy — to live beyond such tribal identities, to construct a society based on the individual, to see ourselves as citizens of a people's republic, to place religion off-limits, and even in recent years to embrace a multiracial and post-religious society — was always an extremely precarious endeavor. It rested, from the beginning, on an 18th-century hope that deep divides can be bridged by a culture of compromise, and that emotion can be defeated by reason. It failed once, spectacularly, in the most brutal civil war any Western democracy has experienced in modern times. And here we are, in an equally tribal era, with a deeply divisive president who is suddenly scrambling Washington's political alignments, about to find out if we can prevent it from failing again...

...When three core components of a tribal identity — race, religion, and geography — define your political parties, you're in serious trouble."[17]

Certain beliefs that we hold only affect us. If I like Italian food and not Chinese, or action movies and not comedies, it's no skin off your back. But with certain topics, namely politics, religion and race, if my belief is in opposition to the next guy's, he might feel threatened and get defensive. If someone doesn't believe climate change exists, or that we should withdraw from the Paris climate accords, that person's views are not just different but, in my opinion, dead wrong and harmful to *my* world. And I will have trouble overlooking that in any interpersonal interactions.

In an Op-Ed for the Times, Thomas Edsall quoted Alex Theodoritis, "Partisanship for many Americans today takes the form of a visceral, even subconscious, attachment to a party group. Our party becomes a part of our self-concept in deep and meaningful ways."[18] David Brooks explains, "For years, the meritocratic establishments in both parties told an implicit myth. The heroes of this myth were

[17] Sullivan, Andrew. "America Wasn't Built for Humans." New York Magazine, 9/19/17.

[18] Edsall, Thomas. "The Party of Lincoln Is Now the Party of Trump." New York Times Op-Ed, 10/26/17.

educated, morally enlightened global citizens who went to competitive colleges, got invited to things like the Clinton Global Initiative, and who have the brainpower to run society and who might just be a little better than other people, by virtue of their achievements. Donald Trump tells the opposite myth — about how those meritocrats are actually clueless idiots and full of drivel, and how virtue, wisdom and toughness is found in the regular people whom those folks look down upon."[19] So the well-educated intellectuals are despised by the anti-intellectuals and their respective echo chambers harden.

The more central a topic is to our *self-image* or identity, the less likely we will be to want to or be able to change. Frequently it is embarrassing when other people know that we have allowed ourselves to be swayed into switching our opinion about an issue. We are afraid of appearing weak or wishy-washy, so we don't give in to other people's attempts to convince us and we stick to our guns. No one wants to look foolish, and most of us need to "save face."

The existence of echo chambers also carries implications for what goes on in psychotherapy. When an adult enters therapy to alleviate insecurities rooted in a poor self-image, what we are talking about are long- and strongly-held beliefs that are central to the person's echo chamber. Changing those beliefs is

19 Brooks, David. "When Politics Becomes Your Idol." New York Times Op-Ed, 10/30/17.

the task of the therapeutic interaction. Echo chambers in therapy will be dealt with in greater detail at a later point.

Another raison d'être for a person's echo chamber is to provide us with workable, and sometimes pleasant, behavioral results. If it ain't broke, why fix it? We choose an action which pleases us, which works for us, which becomes a "habit," and we stick to it. Why not? We have our favorite foods, our preferred mode of dress, our favorite television shows and hobbies. It's who *we* are.

Age may play a factor. When young, we're more open to trying new things. As we mature, we know which choices make us feel good, and there are less "new things" to try since we've already tried most of them. Why should we take a chance on a new entree at our favorite restaurant or a new route to our sister's house since our usual choices work just fine, thank you?

Additionally, establishing patterns of beliefs and behavior helps us to not think so much and not forget things. A morning routine rarely varies. It may involve, in order, using the toilet, showering, brushing ones teeth, shaving, combing hair, etc. If the routine is interrupted confusion may result. We may forget one of the twenty things that we do in sequence. The links between repeated morning activities are similar to listening to a favorite CD. When one song stops, you begin singing the next one in your head.

So far the beliefs that make up our individual echo chambers are buffered by the length of their existence, by the emotional valence and by their relationship to our self-image. They continue because they make our life simpler and allow us to enjoy the things in life that please us. They serve our self-interest in all of these ways.

Chapter 4: How Echo Chambers Process Information

What happens when we encounter events on television that happen in the world outside of our heads? Let's use the topic of immigration as an example. Thoughts about immigrants summon up political beliefs, personal experiences, and biases. Each one of us differs. Some of the possibilities:

> If I believe that immigrants take jobs away from people like me, I am more likely to want them excluded and/or deported.

> If I believe that diversity is good for society, I am more likely to accept immigration and immigrants.

> If I am very pro law and order, illegal immigration bothers me more than legal immigration.

> If I hear about crimes committed by the "other," I am likely to fear them and want them gone from our country.

> If I am raised with liberal values, or am well-educated, I am more likely to accept immigrants.

If I believe that terrorism and immigration are linked, I am likely to be anti-immigrant.

If my parents immigrated to this country in the last fifty years, I am more likely to be pro-immigrant.

Given that we are all prejudiced by degrees, the more I am prejudiced against minorities, the more likely I am to be anti-immigrant.

What appears to happen, within each of us separately, is that the beliefs that we hold internally, somehow *combine* with the topic of immigration, to produce opinions, thoughts and occasionally behaviors (voting, protesting, proselytizing) about whatever event we are currently viewing.

It is believed that what guides and determines how internal beliefs combine with external events are *deductive and inductive logical processes*. It is believed that we either *deduce* new concepts by combining ones that we already hold with what we observe in the world (Democrats suck, Hillary is a Democrat, therefore Hillary sucks, or All people who like Hillary suck, John Doe supports Hillary, therefore John Doe sucks) or we *induce* information from what we observe in the outside world (John is for gun control, so he is most likely a Democrat, or John is a Democrat, so he is most likely for gun control).

It is assumed that most people are logical and make rational decisions most of the time. This is not the same as saying that their conclusions are accurate or true. For example,

> If all men are mortal,
> And Socrates is a man,
> Then Socrates must be mortal.

No one will argue that the conclusion is logical as well as true. But what about...

> If all men are elephants,
> And Socrates is a man,
> Then Socrates must be an elephant.

Uh-oh! Same flawless logic, but operating on a false premise; that "all men are elephants." In a way, this is a metaphor for all human thinking. We can all be logical creatures but if we start out with false (or different) premises (or beliefs) we will end up with false (or different) conclusions. As a computer might say (if it could talk), "garbage in, garbage out." *In real life, most premises aren't true or false, they are just matters of opinion.* Think of choice of car, favorite food, Democrat/Republican.

Here's an important example: If one person believes that life begins at the moment of conception, then abortion is killing. If another believes that life begins at the moment of birth, abortion is not killing. Given a belief one way or the other, conclusions are logically reached, again, one way or the other. We humans walk around with networks of premises in our heads and put them together in a logical way to come to new thoughts and choose behaviors. Behaviors are the conclusions to syllogisms that are observable.

Since each of us thinks logically, but operates on a different subset of premises about a particular subject, we will often reach differing conclusions. To the extent our premises differ, so will our conclusions be at odds. Unfortunately, it is quite common for one person to deem another person's conclusions, which are opinions, as wrong, crazy, stupid, irrational, malicious, or some combination thereof. Note that if I believe John's conclusions are crazy, that statement says something about me. I must hold a belief similar to "You have to be crazy to believe in X. Since John believes in X, he's crazy."

In other cases we use *inductive* logic to come to our conclusions. If I am a minority and grow up hearing about police mistreating people that look like me, I am more likely to think that all police behave that way to all minorities. (This is really a personal statement of probability based on anecdotal evidence.) If I have been turned down for dates by a few young ladies, I may assume that I will always be turned down leading me to isolate myself to avoid the pain and embarrassment. (This is also a statement of probability but the avoider may not be taking into account his own behavior in inducing his conclusion. For example, if he smokes and smells of it, that may be the primary reason for rejection.) In both cases the conclusions may be wrong, but they were *induced* from observed behavior.

In effect, it is logical thinking that helps us maintain our echo chamber. If I am a Republican (or Democrat) and a staunch supporter of the Second Amendment, I will avoid, discount and disagree with any arguments for gun control that are pushed at me by news or social media. That particular part of my echo chamber will remain unchanged.

I will also try to keep my beliefs and constructs consistent because I don't want to think of myself, or be seen by others, as a hypocrite. If information is out there that threatens my belief about the right to bear arms, such as when guns were used in the mass murder of children in Newtown, CT, I will call in other constructs (from within my nexus of beliefs) to maintain consistency. Thus the killer was obviously mentally ill, so what happened in Newtown is a mental health problem, not a Second Amendment issue. Or that the tragedy could have been avoided if school personnel were allowed to bear arms on the premises. Or that we have to accept occasional rare events such as what happened in Newtown because making gun control laws even a little stricter (banning automatic weapons and/or tightening background checks) is a slippery slope which cannot be tolerated. Or after the church shooting in Texas that took twenty-six lives, gun advocates pointed to the fact that "a good guy with a gun got the bad guy with a gun." Playing "devil's advocate," that may be true, but it ignores the primary problem…access to automatic weapons. To which a gun supporter would counter… yes, but "soon they'll be coming after all of our guns." By pulling in these other constructs, my echo chamber remains both intact and consistent.

These other supportive constructs that exist within my echo chamber got there because of the *basic character of all echo chambers: to ingest compatible pieces of information and reject counter examples.* Thus, over the years, I may have "accumulated" beliefs having to do with mass shootings being mental health issues, or school personnel should carry, or "it's a slippery slope."

Maintaining consistency within our echo chambers allows us to staunchly defend our beliefs in the face of contradictory information. Michelle Goldberg noted that despite news coming out in late October 2017 about Trump's campaign staff being implicated in bad behavior, that support for the President was not likely to change.

> "The desire to think the best of Mr. Trump combined with the deep distaste for

Democrats grants extraordinary power to two phrases: 'fake news' and 'the other side is worse.' 'Fake news' erects a shield of disbelief against the worst allegations and allows a person to believe that Mr. Trump is better than he is. For too many Republicans, every single troubling element of the Russia investigation — including multiple administration falsehoods about contacts with Russian officials — represents 'fake news.'[20]

Goldberg recalled an incident at her church,

"People know that I opposed both Mr. Trump and Mrs. Clinton. They often ask what I think of the president's performance. My standard response: I like some things, I dislike others, but I really wish he showed better character. I don't want him to lie. I said this to a sweet older lady not long ago, and she responded — in all sincerity — 'You mean Trump lies?' 'Yes,' I replied. 'All the time.' She didn't answer with a defense. She didn't say 'fake news.' We'd known each other for years, and she trusted my words.

20 French, David. "Mueller's Investigation Won't Shake Trump's Base." New York Times, Op-Ed, 10/30/17.

For a moment, she seemed troubled. I wanted to talk more — to say that we can appreciate and applaud the good things he does, but we can't ignore his flaws, we can't defend his sins, and we can't let him define the future of the Republican Party.

But just then, her jaw set. I saw a flare of defiance in her eyes. She took a sip of coffee, looked straight at me, and I knew exactly what was coming next:

'Well, the Democrats are worse.'"[21]

Goldberg points out that Trump supporters usually start their defense by invoking the "fake news" preferred by the liberal media. If and when faced with irrefutable evidence that the news was not fake or that Trump lied, then they pull "the other side is worse" meme out of their pockets.

Corollary beliefs allow a person to maintain consistency within his or her echo chamber. If a Trump supporter believes John McCain or Jeff Flake or MSNBC when they called out Trump for some outrageous lie or offensive action, it would be hard for them to keep supporting him. But if they believe that his opponents are spreading fake news about him, they can continue to support him and, in fact, get angry at his opponents. Trotting out the assertion of

[21] ibid.

"fake news" or that "the other side is worse" allows their echo chambers to remain consistent and pro-Trump.

Chapter 5: Motivation Within Echo Chambers

If deductive and inductive logic describes the processes that go on within our echo chambers, what is the motivator behind these processes? It is believed that by far the most important motivator, perhaps the only one, is self-interest in various forms. The study of self-interest, and the way it pervades our lives is called "Selfonomics." A complete discussion can be found in "Selfonomics: How Broadly-Defined Self-Interest Explains Everything" by this author.[22]

As a rule, perceived self-interest motivates all of us, all the time. It involves anything that makes us feel good, or helps us to feel less bad. If it involves assertively filling our needs, makes us feel better, or involves pleasure seeking behavior, it is called *Direct Self-Interest*, or DSI. If it involves protection from, or avoidance of, negative feelings, real or imagined, it is called *Protective Self-Interest*, or PSI. Note that perceived self-interest may not *actually* be to our benefit, as in drinking too much or speeding to get somewhere to avoid being late. Or a behavior that starts out as being in our self-interest, such as having a drink or two at a party can, over time, lead to alcoholism, which is definitely *not* in our self-interest.

---

[22] Gribin, Anthony J. <u>Selfonomics: How Broadly-Defined Self-Interest Explains Everything.</u> 2014: ttgPress.

Any type of self-interest can be quite misguided.[23]

All of the beliefs that occupy our echo chamber are in the service of what *we believe* is in our self-interest. This perceived self-interest may get us what we want or protect us from something we don't want. It may actually be good for us, or be misguided. Self-interest, biological or cognitive, guides, constrains, focuses and determines the content of our echo chamber; the nexus of beliefs that we hold.

Self-interest is benevolent, justifiable, idiosyncratic and not necessarily conscious. It is benevolent in that we ordinarily do not intend harm to anyone except when we are defending ourselves (which is protective self-

---

[23] There are two important examples of Protective Self-Interest in the news simultaneously in the fall of 2017. On MSNBC Nicolle Wallace's news program on November 29, 2017 panelists, including Tara Setemeyer and William Kristol were wondering why some politicians don't have the "cojones" to come out against the outrageous things that Donald Trump says or tweets. On this day, he re-tweeted three anti-Muslim messages originally posted by a white supremacist group from England. The day before he called Elizabeth Warren "Pocahontas" (again) in front of a group of elderly native American code talkers in the Oval office and smack in front of a portrait of Andrew Jackson. The result was a double racial slur against Native Americans. The short reason for the silence of Republican congresspeople is that they are afraid they will be out of a job.

The same exact fear, that of losing a job, is what keeps many women from coming forward after being sexually harassed. Thus both politicians and harassed women who keep silent are motivated by PSI. Is this misguided PSI? One can argue either way, but the politicians are selling their souls and the women are, in effect, accepting the shame or guilt or long term emotional consequences that come with keeping quiet. And both are enabling perpetrators.

interest). It is justifiable in that we always have what we see as legitimate reasons for doing or saying what we did or said. It is idiosyncratic in that we all live in our own unique echo chambers which contain our own favorite ways of thinking, speaking and acting. And what motivates us is self-interest that is not necessarily in conscious thought but is almost always retrievable so that we can give reasons for why we did what we did. These reasons might not be totally accurate all the time,[24] but they will be close.

If one wants proof of the centrality of self-interest to our existence, one only need look at evolution. As we have evolved as a species, those with better survival instincts lived to reproduce. Those whose survival instincts were less well developed, perished. Early humans spent almost all of their time hunting and gathering food, providing shelter, tending to their family, defending their brood from predators, human and otherwise, and not much else. Self-interest was clear and uncomplicated; survival.

Survival involved both direct and protective self-interest. The strongest, fastest and wiliest humans (and perhaps the most physically appealing) caught and killed more game, ate better, were the leaders of their

_____

[24] Some reasons for the inaccuracy are not wanting to admit our selfish thoughts or actions even to ourselves, having a confluence of many reasons for what we did and not recognizing all of them, and outright lying so as to not hurt or anger someone else.

tribes and reproduced more easily (other things being equal). That's DSI. But what about PSI?

Survival requires both offense and defense. The better a human protected himself and his brood from becoming food for another organism, the better the odds of survival and procreation. Both DSI and PSI have to be operating for each species for it to survive and, on the other extreme, in balance with other species so as not to take over the world.

Survival has been honed into the DNA of every species, ever. Primitive organisms that had more of a "self-interest drive" built into their DNA, meaning they were better suited to compete for resources, survived to reproduce; the meek, or those that were the poorer hunters or less able defenders, perished. If we subscribe to the theory of evolution, by definition, our DNA has evolved to support self-interest. Over the millennia, perhaps the ratio of the use of brain power to the use of physical strength has changed a little, but otherwise things are not much different.

Almost all humans that have ever lived worked hard and long to satisfy the most basic of needs of food, clothing and shelter. Even throughout the last several thousand years, most were illiterate, poor and overworked. Only the cream of society had access to the finer things in life and the time to appreciate them. And these elite acted in their own self-interest as well, if only to maintain their privileged positions. Although today most humans can look well beyond food and shelter, the self-interest motive doesn't appear to have changed much in modern times. The average person of the twenty-first century will still be faced with physical needs, as well as safety needs and desires to be social and respected within their communities. All of these speak to, and are driven by, self-interest.

One potential speed bump for a theory of all-pervasive self-interest is how do we account for parent-child love, where most parents put their children before themselves? It is explained by assuming that we see our children as *extensions or parts of ourselves,* looking out for them *as if they were us.* On an evolutionary basis, those parents who protected/loved their children more continued to advance their blood lines, while those nuclear families with weaker parental instincts died out.[25]

Parents look out for their children as they do for themselves until the children are ready to take over that job. To that end, parents teach their children how to take care of themselves, how to defend themselves, and how not to let others take advantage of them. They teach the skills needed to survive in the society in which they will grow up. They also instill rules that are necessary to curb their own feral, unbridled self-interest. Thus we learn to brush our teeth, eat

---

25 Dawkins, R. (2006). The Selfish Gene (30th Anniversary Edition). New York City: Oxford University Press.

vegetables, get enough sleep, attend school, as well as take turns, be polite, and do unto others as we would have them do unto us.

We are not born knowing *not* to steal. We learn parameters to govern our self-interest; that is, it is okay to want something, but we must say, "please" to get it and "thank you" after we get it. These magic words help disguise self-interest and hide it from both the asker and the one asked. Rules, primarily taught by parents, curb, direct and guide our instinctive self-interest. In fact, learning these rules and guidelines actually improves the chance, over the long run, that we'll get what we want.

Taken altogether, direct and protective self-interest within nuclear families, supported tribalism from the beginning of the human (and much animal) existence. Members of a family and of the greater tribe looked out for and protected each other. The ones that did this best passed on their genes. As has been said, it is "survival of the fittest."

In modern society, self-interest is not as obvious as hunting, gathering and fighting off predators. Self-interest is often displayed in subtle ways. Some examples:

Saving face. This is Protective Self-Interest in the service of our ego. If we are caught in a lie, it is sometimes difficult to admit it, because we look foolish. On occasion we are tempted to tell another lie, to cover the first, in order to "save face." Saving face can also be an important part of compromise. That is, both sides need to get something out of a negotiation so that they won't look like a "loser."

Keeping a job, whether in Congress or anywhere else. Sometimes people go against their principles because if they don't they will be voted out of office. This is particularly true in modern gerrymandered congressional districts. Of course this applies, as has been described before, to women who are afraid to come forward with accusations of sexual harassment. It also provides a reason for Congresspeople starting to fundraise almost immediately after being installed, since the next election is only two years away. Their careers depend upon it. These examples are Direct Self-Interest.

Kissing ass. A good recent example of this is the sycophancy demonstrated by appointees of President Trump. Mike Pence, our Vice President, recently groveled, "I'm deeply humbled, as your vice president, to be able to be here...You've restored American credibility on the world stage...You've spurred an optimism in this country that's setting records."[26] This is what seems to happen at Trump's cabinet meetings; members compete to see who can humble themselves the most. These genuflections may be in the direct self-interest of the participants, but are seen by many outside observers as misguided to the point of being laughable.[27]

Keeping your head down. Not volunteering or not raising your hand in class, not "squealing" on a friend, or literally keeping your head down in a foxhole are all examples of Protective Self-Interest.

Remaining in your echo chamber. This almost goes without saying. If I seek and ingest only information with which I am comfortable, I experience less dissonance and get less upset, serving either Direct (rooting for "my side") and/or Protective (not

---

[26] Waldman, Katy. "A Flight of Sycophancy: A line-by-line breakdown of Mike Pence's master class in toadyism." Slate, 12/21/17. At: http://www.slate.com/articles/news_and_politics/politics/2017/12/
a_line_by_line_breakdown_of_mike_pence_s_master_class_in_toadyism.html

[27] Merriam-Webster defines "sycophant" as "a servile self-seeking flatterer." Not something to which one should aspire, given that synonyms include lackey, bootlicker, brown-noser and parasite. An "appeaser" is one who makes "concessions to (someone, such as an aggressor or a critic) often at the sacrifice of principles." The word "enabler," in recent years identified with substance abuse, is defined as "one who enables another to persist in self-destructive behavior by providing excuses or by making it possible to avoid the consequences of such behavior." Donald Trump only surrounds himself with sycophants who appease and enable him.

feeling my blood rise in reaction to information from the "other side") Self-Interest.

Chapter 6: Behavioral Data Points

To summarize to this point: We've posited that each of us is an echo chamber, in the sense that we seek information that is consistent with what we believe, and dismiss or ignore information that is contradictory. The nexus of beliefs within us is buffered, meaning that the longer we've held a belief, the more resistant it will be to change.

The beliefs within our echo chamber will be more resistant to change the more we have an emotional investment in them and the more they involve our self-image. The beliefs help us form routines which make our lives simpler so that we don't have to think did about every action anew. We develop a catalog of preferences which guide the enjoyable stuff and keep us from things we have tried and disliked.

Inside our echo chamber, inductive and deductive logic operates to combine our existing beliefs with new information that emanates from the outside. Although the process is logical, the truth or falsity of the conclusions we draw depend on the accuracy of the premises. We can logically deduce inaccurate information if we start with false premises.

What motivates our thoughts and eventually our actions, is self-interest designed to further our needs and wants, and protect us from untoward events or consequences. Our self-interest, as perceived by us, can either work for us or, if misguided, work against us.

An outside observer cannot see the contents of another person's echo chamber, or the logic or motivations that guide it. The only thing that can be observed is that person's behavior. Since the other guy's echo chamber provides internal consistency for him, the outward manifestations will be observable to us as "data points." It is these data points that allow us to describe an individual's "personality."

Suppose you see your neighbor Joe doing chores around the house every weekend. You call him to play golf with you, and he thanks you, but declines, saying that he has a lot of chores to do. Your wife calls his to ask if they'd like to go out to dinner with you as a couple. They politely decline. They also don't come to neighborhood barbecues occasionally thrown by people in the community. These are all data points which might lead you to surmise that Joe and his wife, though polite and nice, are shy or antisocial, and/or are just homebodies. Or perhaps they don't like you. Those data points define them.

Or, you frequently see Jill at various neighborhood get-togethers. Each time she seems to drink too much and ends up slurring her words. You also notice that her husband seems upset and makes excuses for her behavior. You might conclude that Jill is an alcoholic and her husband is an enabler.

Or you have a friend Leo, who is never on time,

sometimes cancels meetings at the last minute, and often seems to have an on-again, off-again relationship with the truth. You notice, in your increasingly infrequent interactions with him, that the Leo-pard doesn't change his spots. You should have Leo's number and if you don't, it's your bad.

Or, in the public sphere, one male seems to be always in the headlines with a series of women, often being accused of improper behavior. (Think Bill Clinton, Bill Cosby, Donald Trump, Harvey Weinstein.)[28] Each new imbroglio is not likely to be a coincidence.

Politicians, because they are so often in the headlines, are quite easy to pigeonhole. Five examples are Mitt Romney, Chris Christie, Hillary Clinton, Donald Trump and Mike Pence. When Romney ran for President in 2012, he made numerous statements that attracted the attention of the media, especially left-leaning media. His (paraphrased) comments such as, "I only made $250,000 from my book," "I'll bet you $10,000" to rival Rick Perry, "My wife has two Cadillac Escalades," "My house in California has an elevator for cars," "I don't have to worry about the 47% of the people who will vote for the President" and, of course, the discovery that as a youth he was the ringleader of a group of boys at an exclusive prep school that bullied another student and took a scissors

---

28 Since the first draft of this section, the names Kevin Spacey, Roy Moore and Al Franken can be added, among several others.

to his long hair. It would not be unreasonable for one to induce from these behaviors that Romney was out of touch with the common man. Most people don't act or talk like that.

Chris Christie's behavior indicates a person who is comfortable being a bully. Kate Zernike's article in the New York Times from December 2013[29], describes situations where people in power lost their jobs, their police escort, their funding, all for having crossed Christie in some minor way or even just disagreed with him. In late October, 2014, he told a protester, "Sit down and shut up!" Not that he was wrong in what he said. But the way he said it and his choice of words and vehemence indicate his style. And of course, there was the "Bridgegate" scandal, in which traffic jams were created in retribution for not supporting Christie's reelection, which got national attention. Although it may be that Christie did not order the traffic jam himself, the cultural climate created by him allowed and perhaps encouraged others to do it.

Hillary Clinton comes off, at least in public, as quite competent and dedicated but lacking in warmth. Republicans have also labeled her as "untrustworthy," dwelling on her email practices, Whitewater and Benghazi. The absence of warmth problem is one that she and other women encounter when they are strong and not goofy (as was Sarah Palin). The same

---

29 Zernike, Kate. "Christie Worried About Bridge Scandal, Report Finds." New York Times, 12/5/13.

behavior that is esteemed in men is an Achilles heel for women. That exact reputation followed Carly Fiorina, Christine Whitman and Condoleeza Rice. Angela Merkl, Margaret Thatcher and Golda Meir would have struck out if they had been in American politics.

Donald Trump's data points have been on display since he began his campaign for the Presidency. His narcissism, difficulty with telling the truth, thin skin, ruthless counterpunching, absence of civility, disdain for tradition, need for flattery and praise, preoccupation with winning, among other similar traits, define him quite clearly. Just about every one of his statements and actions reveals these attitudes. This is his echo chamber, his personality, that predictably leads him to, for example, viciously attack anyone, weak or strong, that is critical of him. His echo chamber is remarkably consistent implying that it is also remarkably rigid.

Even bland people, such as Vice President Mike Pence display consistent behavioral data points.

> "Pence can sound insipid on any topic.
> When the tape emerged last year of Trump
> boasting about how to be a sexual
> predator and get away with it, Pence
> urged his ticket mate to pray. His piety is
> the cover for Trump's amorality... Pence
> calls himself a Christian first, a

conservative second and a Republican third. Since taking the oath of office, he's supposed to be a citizen first. But Pence is a theocrat — one who hasn't had a new thought in years — and that's why he sounds so vacuous…Pence learned gasbagging for God as a talk-radio host, calling himself 'Rush Limbaugh on decaf.' It's a job that requires someone to fill hours of empty air with hours of empty nonsense. As vice president, he has refined the role."[30]

The examples above illustrate the way people's echo chambers are revealed by a fairly consistent set of behaviors which we are calling data points. The echo chambers of the real people in our lives are likely to be more mundane though just as consistent and intractable. One is consistently a neatnik, one reliably messy, one a sports nut, one an intellectual, one a rabid conservative, one a bleeding liberal. We all show our echo chambers through our choices, words and behaviors. The data points we observe about another person are what we use to describe their "personality."

---

[30] Egan, Timothy. "The Vacuity of the Vice President." New York Times Op-Ed. 11/10/17.

Chapter 7: The Diversity of Echo Chambers

Information has exploded since the arrival of the internet and related technologies. In the 1950s, the "Ozzie and Harriet" and "Father Knows Best" television shows represented the type of family to which most people aspired. Everyone watched one of three major networks and the same popular programs such as "I Love Lucy," "Gunsmoke" and "The Ed Sullivan Show." We listened to one of a handful of radio stations operating within the reach of our antennas and played standards or rock & roll, got the news from one of only a few sources (ABC, NBC, CBS, Walter Cronkite, Huntley & Brinkley, and a few local newspapers), liked all-American foods (hot dogs and hamburgers, apple pie, Kraft Cheese, pizza, americanized Chinese food), bought American cars, had very similar goals (children, house with the white picket fence). Not that we felt that our choices were restricted or suffered as a result of those restrictions. That was just the way things were.

Think about how the range and scope of available media and lifestyle choices has expanded in the last sixty years. There are almost unlimited choices for genres of music, television shows, sources of news, varieties of foods, lifestyles (gay/trans/bi/straight), and even cultures. Our population is much more diverse, not only in skin color and language, but in sources of influence, preferences and occupations. All of which means that the echo chambers of the members of our society will be much more unique than ever before. We may have less in common with our neighbor than with someone across the world.

I was recently on vacation with my wife in the area of Lake George, N.Y. We are not wealthy, but we are fairly comfortable, and every once in a while can splurge on a nice hotel such as the Sagamore in Boltons Landing, N.Y. As we were driving around the lake we passed a slew of less expensive, less attractive places to stay. It was August and many of them seemed well-populated, some even had pools with children swimming and laughing therein. I thought that my wife and I would not enjoy staying at one of these places. And yet, it was obvious that many others would, did and thoroughly enjoyed themselves.

Are our echo chambers similar to those of the people who stay at those places? We wouldn't eat the (assumed non-health-conscious) food they enjoyed, wouldn't want to sleep on those (assumed) lumpy beds, and probably wouldn't have much to talk about with many of the people that stayed there. And they would probably see us as rich and spoiled and intellectually snobbish.[31] Maybe we are. But these differences are not as severe or dramatic as some of the ones that exist in the larger universe.

---

[31] It may be that the motel-ers and hotel-ers have quite a few things in common, but they are far from obvious.

Another factor in diversity is the change in the social fabric. Compare today to the 1950s. Then, there was much less divorce and fewer children of divorce, closer ties, both emotionally and geographically to family, more reverence for family elders, more job (and thus financial) security, more time spent as a family at dinners and in front of the only screen in the home. With more divorce comes emotional upheaval for both parents and children. Hollowing out of the middle class means more worry about finances and job security. Living further away from parents and grandparents means they influence our life less and are less likely to share our beliefs. Core family values may be up for grabs and the more outlandish memes may attract us. Stories that used to be laughed at when they appeared in the National Enquirer (a supermarket tabloid) are now fodder for extremist groups.

Going further, how can someone who often doesn't have enough to eat, or who has lost a job and can't support his/her family, or who grows up around addiction or crime think the same way as someone who has a "normal" life?[32] That is, a life where at least one family member has a secure job, where no one goes hungry, where there are no obvious addictions and minimal crime? How can someone who didn't do well in or didn't value school, who doesn't read very

[32] Vance, J.D. Hillbilly Elegy: A Memoir of a Family and Culture in Crisis. Harper Collins, 2016.

much, who prefers sports, or soap operas or crime dramas, who doesn't pay attention to news, have a reasonable grasp of what is going on in the world?

A person who rarely reads about, hears or watches the news can't have a deep understanding of world issues. One can't tune in once in a while to a news program and understand what is going on. Many issues are complex (immigration, taxation, health care, racism) and there is a context which will be missed with occasional viewing. The issues are more evolving stories than discrete events (natural disasters and mass killings perhaps being exceptions). Not knowing what is going on makes one receptive to sound bites or one liners such as "Make America Great Again" or "Crooked Hillary" or "Obamacare is a disaster." How can a person with limited knowledge of world events and issues have much in common with someone who grows up to value education, reading and keeping up with current events?

These people will have a totally different nexus of beliefs; totally different echo chambers. News that affects, either positively or negatively, someone who is tuned in, is totally off the radar screen of the person who is tuned out. They could almost be from different parts of the world, or perhaps just not speak the same language. In fact, not speaking the same language is an appropriate analogy.

But here's the rub. People don't like to admit ignorance or be told that they are wrong. So they grasp onto news that provides "shiny objects"; news that attracts their attention because it is sensationalistic, and/or is delivered in an entertaining way by a showman (perhaps shaman is a better term), without regard to its accuracy. This is where *real* "fake news"[33] comes in. Educated and tuned-in people can and do disagree on the issues, but will not resort to "alternative facts" without a malicious intent. The ignorant or uninterested will grab onto the shiny news objects, that when taken in by their echo chamber and acted on logically, will produce false conclusions. Remember… garbage in, garbage out.

The echo chambers of some individuals contain super-ordinating constructs that occupy a central place in their nexus of beliefs and set them apart from others. People without these constructs may have difficulty in understanding their positions. I am a non-religious Jew. I grew up in a predominantly Jewish neighborhood and went to a college with a large proportion of Jewish students (City College of New York). The only time I felt disliked because of my religion was when I was living off campus at S.U.N.Y. at Albany graduate school. The landlord, as I found out, didn't like Jews, so I switched living arrangements and that was that. So on a personal level, I almost never felt prejudice.

But among Jews more invested in the religion,

---

[33] A bit of an oxymoron.

there is a continual need to be alert to signs of anti-semitism. Remembering that we are all in our own echo chambers, those that are closer to the religion are more exposed to stories of anti-semitic activities throughout the world. To me, it seems a bit foreign, but I understand how being exposed to news of antisemitic incidents would put people on frequent, if not constant, alert.

My personal experience with prejudice, however slight, makes me want to try to put myself in the place of other minorities. For example, what must the echo chamber of an African American be like? If I were African American, and among my own, I would feel comfortable, yet news of racial bias would be commonly exchanged between and among us, keeping my antennae up. If I were among caucasians, I might be frequently on alert. Are they friendly or hostile? Do they accept me as an equal or do they see me as "less than?" Are they racially prejudiced?[34] Are they haters?

An eloquent description of a black man's view of the situation was offered by Ekow N. Yankah:

> "It is impossible to convey the mixture of heartbreak and fear I feel for [my sons]. Donald Trump's election has made it clear that I will teach my boys the lesson

---

[34] It is recognized that we are all prejudiced by degrees.

generations old, one that I for the most part nearly escaped. I will teach them to be cautious, I will teach them suspicion, and I will teach them distrust. Much sooner than I thought I would, I will have to discuss with my boys whether they can truly be friends with white people.

Meaningful friendship is not just a feeling. It is not simply being able to share a beer. Real friendship is impossible without the ability to trust others, without knowing that your well-being is important to them. The desire to create, maintain or wield power over others destroys the possibility of friendship. The Rev. Dr. Martin Luther King Jr.'s famous dream of black and white children holding hands was a dream precisely because he realized that in Alabama, conditions of dominance made real friendship between white and black people impossible...

...But the deepest rift is with the apologists, the 'good' Trump voters, the white people who understand that Mr. Trump says 'unfortunate' things but support him because they like what he says on jobs and taxes. They bristle at the accusation that they supported racism, insisting they had to ignore Mr. Trump's ugliness. Relying on everyday decency as a shield, they are befuddled at the chill that now separates them from black people in their offices and social circles. They protest: Have they ever said anything racist? Don't they shovel the sidewalk of the new black neighbors? Surely, they say, politics — a single vote — does not mean we can't be friends."[35]

Another well-respected author's echo chamber offers a rather sad view of how African-Americans view the white world. What follows is Andrew Sullivan's description of the views of Ta-Nehisi Coates:

"He remains a vital voice, but in more recent years, a somewhat different one. His mood has become much gloomier. He calls the Obama presidency a 'tragedy,' and describes many Trump supporters as 'not so different from those same Americans who grin back at us in lynching photos.' He's written about how watching cops and firefighters enter the smoldering World Trade Center instantly reminded him of cops mistreating blacks: They 'were

[35] Yankah, Ekow N. "Can My Children Be Friends With White People?" New York Times, Sunday Review, 11/11/17.

not human to me.' In his latest essay in the Atlantic, analyzing why Donald Trump won the last election, he dismisses any notion that economic distress might have played a role as 'empty' and ignores other factors, such as Hillary Clinton's terrible candidacy, the populist revolt against immigration that had become a potent force across the West, and the possibility that the pace of social change might have triggered a backlash among traditionalists. No, there was one meaningful explanation only: white supremacism. And those who accept, as I do, that racism was indeed a big part of the equation but also saw other factors at work were simply luxuriating in our own white privilege because we are never under 'racism's boot.'"[36][37]

It is noted that some African Americans are more attuned than others to reactions from whites. Some will feel anxiety, others anger or disgust, again by degrees. For Charles Blow, an Op-Ed columnist for the New York Times, anger seeps through his words:

---

[36] Sullivan, Andrew. op cit.

[37] Coates, Ta-Nehisi. "The First White President." The Atlantic, October, 2017. https://www.theatlantic.com/magazine/archive/2017/10/the-first-white-president-ta-nehisi-coates/537909/

"For me, there is no middle: If you are supporting Donald Trump, you are supporting Trumpism and all that goes with it. That means that you are supporting a modus operandi that attacks people of color on every term, but keeps white supremacists safe. You are supporting Trump's demeaning of women. You are supporting his bullying. You are supporting his corruption. You are supporting his pathological lying."[38]

Many will not trust.[39] It will depend, in part, on their own experiences with caucasians, on what they've heard from peers, on what they were taught at home, school and in church, and to which sources of news they subscribe. In any of these cases, the construct of being a minority in a predominantly white society is likely to occupy a central place in their echo chambers. It also predicts that African Americans, in fact all discrete groups including Jews, Muslims, Hispanics, etc., will tend to self-segregate, since they feel more comfortable around and among their own and have to be less "on guard." (It is

---

38 Blow, Charles. "Resistance, for the Win!" New York Times Op-Ed, 11/9/17.

39 These same statements will be true of whites, vis a vis blacks.

realized that this will occur by degrees and will not be the rule for everyone.)

Similar arguments can be made for other minorities. Imagine the way an LGBTQ person, or an immigrant, or a Muslim must view the world in the United States in 2018. Again, in their element or within their family, their identity won't be much of an issue. But out in the larger world, the construct of identity must play a major part of the way they filter events as they are sucked into their echo chambers. Even distinct groups that are not in the minority, such as women, may keep their gender at the center of the way they see the world in certain circumstances (for example if they have been sexually harassed or worse).

Adding to diversity, what if we consider wealth, occupation and attractiveness? It would not be surprising if a wealthy person's echo chamber is radically different from someone who is poor, a person who works with his hands is much different from those of an office worker, and a person whose looks are want-ing thinks differently than a beautiful person. Being extreme on any dimension means that whatever quality we're talking about (wealth, occupation, looks) will occupy a more central place in one's echo chamber. And the result of increasing diversity is increased tribalism.

Chapter 8: Adding Technology to the Mix

"The question has to do with how do we
harness this technology in a way that
allows a multiplicity of voices, allows a
diversity of views, but doesn't lead to a
Balkanization of society and allows ways of
finding common ground."

-President Barack Obama, in a BBC interview
conducted by Prince Harry of England, broadcast
on December 27, 2017.

What relationship does advancing technology have on
the content of our echo chambers? Technology, as
discussed here, can include greater ease of travel via
car and plane, advances brought on by digital
telephony and the obvious benefits of computeri-
zation and the internet.

Increasing ease of travel has led to more
intermingling of cultures. Americans can get to Asia
and Europe more easily whether for business or
pleasure; Hispanics and Muslims can get to the United
States to improve their lives; Europeans can travel
freely between nations within the European Union,
etc. Some travelers visit and then go home, but others
stay and settle and eventually intermarry. America is
no longer the almost exclusively white Protestant

country it used to be. Many European countries have accepted an influx of immigrants and refugees from middle Eastern countries. Diversity, in turn, brings differences in belief systems. Americans don't have as much in common with each other as they used to.

Telephony has become easier and less expensive. One would think that being able to talk to friends and relatives at a distance would be neutral to our echo chambers, but there is no such thing as just a phone any more. It is a small computer, which allows us to play games, get news and, in effect, live in our individual silos. Just one more way in which there can be differences among echo chambers. After all, if I play Scrabble and Words With Friends on my phone and you are addicted to violent role playing games, we may not have a lot in common.

Computers have added a sinister dimension. It used to be if one person espoused radical ideas, few people would listen. Aside from shouting his beliefs from the rooftops, there were few ways to effectively disseminate radical and divisive ideas. That person would have little credibility with anyone that knew him (he would be seen as an oddball) and had no way of reaching large numbers of people that didn't know him.

Computers have changed this dynamic. Any guy or gal with a computer and a modicum of skill can set up a website or blog and broadcast anything they choose. If they are not content with their lives, they can attract other malcontents, with similar gripes, to their cause and potentially wreak havoc. This is how ISIS was able to attract so many young people. ISIS is skilled at creating attractive videos and offering an exciting life to (mostly) young men who are unhappy with their own. The ease of posting to social media, including YouTube, makes the spread of violent and sexually explicit material easy. If the content is appealing enough, even in a sadistic kind of way, it may go viral and attract followers to the person that posted it.

Only a small step down in infamy from recruiting for terrorist causes is the proliferation of alt-right media and fake news. It's been documented how someone in a basement in Ukraine or some other remote place has fabricated stories about, as an example, Hillary Clinton, with the express purpose of making money, and how it was rebroadcast and/or tweeted and believed by many.[40][41] Examples are, "FBI agent suspected in Hillary Email leaks found dead in apparent murder-suicide" and "Pope Francis Shocks World, Endorses Donald Trump for President, Releases Statement." These "headlines" are posted on alt-right websites (such as Breitbart) and often end up

[40] Oehlheiser, Amy. "This is how Facebook's fake-news writers make money." Washington Post, 11/18/16.

[41] Fiegerman, Seth. "Facebook's global fight against fake news." CNN Tech, 5/9/17. (http://money.cnn.com/2017/05/09/technology/facebook-fake-news/index.html)

on Facebook being shared thousands of times. Note that unlike "legitimate" news sources, these alt-right outlets seem to omit the step of fact-checking, since if the stories *were* fact checked, they would've proven false. Recently members of Trump's campaign, and even the President himself, retweeted some of this false reportage, lending even more credibility to them. Donald Trump has approximately 40 million followers and if even a fraction of that number believe him, the result is scary.

Retweeting of these unproven and/or false stories, especially by someone in power, can have particularly unwanted consequences. At the end of November, 2017, Donald Trump retweeted three anti-Muslim videos posted by a white supremacist British group.[42] "The first video purportedly shows a 'Muslim migrant' attacking a young Dutch man on crutches. However, the claim in this tweet appears to have little substance. A spokesperson from the Dutch Public Prosecution Service told the BBC that the person arrested for the attack 'was born and raised in the Netherlands' and was not a migrant, as claimed in the social media post."[43] The (hopefully) unintended consequences were that the British government and people were deeply offended, and now have to

---

[42] "Donald Trump retweets far-right group's anti-Muslim videos." BBC News, 11/29/17. http://www.bbc.com/news/world-us-canada-42166663

[43] ibid.

endure the possibility of a backlash from Muslims in the U.K. So for no apparent reason, Trump created a rift between the U.S. and one of their staunchest allies.

All that is required to promote this type of false story is a statement to the effect that "Some people are saying…". It is ironic that the type of stories that appeared in the National Enquirer, ones that used to be fodder for laughter and derision, now can go viral and reach millions of unsuspecting people. Without checking the facts, many are defenseless in the face of this type of "news." An excellent four minute video by a Times reporter provides a summary of how, with advancing technology, the spread of paranoid memes has become so easy.[44]

It appears that technology has also used offensively as a weapon to damage the political system of another country. There is, of course, the evolving story (as of April, 2018) of possible Russian involvement in our election process, using computers in an attempt to hack state races and purchasing adds on Facebook, Google and Twitter to favor one candidate over another. It is probable that our own government is not innocent in this regard either,

---

[44] Hess, Amanda. "How the Internet Fuels Paranoid Thinking." New York Times Video, 11/13/17.https://www.nytimes.com/video/arts/100000005417743/how-the-internet-fuels-paranoid-thinking.html

doubtlessly doing what they can to insinuate the interests of the United States into foreign politics.[45]

Another wrinkle introduced by technology is complexity. We are bombarded by much more information than ever before. We have access to unlimited amounts of data coming from every direction. How do we choose which things to attend to? Choices of television channels provides an instructive example. In the 1950s in New York City, there were three networks and four other channels of lesser importance. Now there are hundreds, if not thousands.

We used to have to go to the local library to do research. Now we have access to the equivalent of thousands of libraries on our own computer. How do we narrow our choices? Our echo chambers help us to filter and slow down the flow of information, but there is a cost. We grasp snippets, memes, glib phrases. "The essence of the problem isn't new: Our brains are prone to turning complex ideas into easy-to-understand tidbits, and social media capitalizes on that. But today's information overload seems to encourage our worst impulses: tribalism, insulation,

---

[45] The radio broadcasting of "Tokyo Rose" in the WWII era was an antecedent of internet interference during World War II, as was Radio Free Europe and Radio Liberty in the late 1940s.

and favoring the quick, digestible version of "truth" over claims that require due diligence."[46]

The problem is that "due diligence" is beyond the reach of most of us since we are not trained to analyze data or news properly and don't have the time to do so. Many of us are not taught to think for ourselves; we are taught to believe. And that makes us susceptible to memes and fake news that we don't, won't or can't factcheck. This may be an exaggeration, but the more information is pushed at us, the more we retreat into our own echo chambers in which, almost by definition, we are most comfortable.

[46] Baraniuk, Chris. "Social media loves echo chambers, but the human brain helps create them." Quartz, 11/17/16. (https://qz.com/839982/social-media-loves-echo-chambers-but-the-human-brain-helps-create-them/)

Chapter 9: False Equivalence

Paul Krugman, Nobel Prize winner in economics and admitted liberal Op-ed writer for the New York Times, once "...joked long ago that if one party declared that the earth was flat, the headlines would read 'Views Differ on Shape of Planet.'"[47] Amusing but scary. And timely.

If the theory that people think logically holds water, then the accuracy or truth of a person's premises is a dead-on indicator of the accuracy or truth of their conclusions. Remember "garbage in, garbage out?"

What happens when someone in the public eye believes in something that is demonstrably false? For example, what if someone doesn't believe that human activity exacerbates climate change? Yes, there are underlying geological variations in temperatures around the globe. But to deny that the result of human activity is an "add-on effect" to geological variation denies science. When agreement among scientists is in the high 90s about the dangers of climate change, and these are the people that were educated to know this stuff, why would anyone listen to contrary information from a person who is outside the world of science and knows nothing about it? Or perhaps gets her input from Facebook?

---

[47] Krugman, Paul. "The Centrist Cop-Out." New York Times Op-Ed, 7/28/11.

Yet an echo chamber holding the belief that climate change is a hoax or doesn't exist can do a lot of damage. If I believe it's a hoax I will enlist corollary constructs to continue to believe what I believe, such as "those scientists just want to keep their jobs," or "it's a Chinese plot," or "you can't trust those intellectual elitists." The deniers, including President Trump and his followers, can lead us to get back into gas-guzzling cars,[48] to pull out of the Paris Climate Accords and to favor pollution-intense means of providing energy. Giving equal weight to both sides of this argument is false equivalence.

Or what about people whose echo chambers contain the belief that "Tax Cuts Do More to Stimulate The Economy Than Food Stamps and Unemployment Benefits."[49] A dollar spent on Unemployment Benefits or Food Stamps creates over a dollar and a half of growth, while a tax cut of a dollar returns just a third in benefits.[50] Note that tax cuts may help, but not as much as directing the cuts elsewhere on the economic ladder. I'm not an economist, but it's clear that if you give someone who is relatively poor a dollar, he will spend it immediately, and the clerk at the 7-11 that he

---

[48] Oge, Marge. "Looser Emissions Standards Will Hurt the Auto Industry." New York Times Op-Ed, 3/30/18.

[49] Cesca, Bob. "Debunking the Top 10 Most Egregious Republican Lies." Huffpost, The Blog, updated 5/24/14.

[50] ibid.

94

gives it to will spend it almost as fast, creating rapidly circulating currency. If you give a dollar to someone who is well-off, he will likely save it or invest it, with the result that the money takes a long time to circulate through the economy.

This argument is particularly cogent as of December of 2017, since a tax reform bill that gives most of the breaks to the very wealthy just passed the Senate by a vote of 51-49.[51] If one believes that a trickle down economy is the way to go, then one can ignore the immediate needs of the poor and middle class because it is believed that the money will eventually get to them. Eventually?

Or how about the assertion that voter fraud is rife. "President Donald Trump has repeatedly, and falsely, claimed millions voted illegally. Yet examination after examination of voter fraud claims reveal fraud is very rare, voter impersonation is nearly non-existent, and many of the problems associated with alleged fraud relates to unintentional mistakes by voters or election administrators. Election officials and leaders of the president's own party also agree fraud is not widespread."[52]

---

[51] "Senate Passes Revision of U.S. Tax Code." Wall Street Journal, 12/2/17.

[52] "Myth of Voter Fraud." Brennan Center for Justice, New York University School of Law. https://www.brennancenter.org/issues/voter-fraud

On their website, the Heritage Foundation, a Conservative Think Tank, counters, "The United States has a long and unfortunate history of election fraud. The Heritage Foundation is providing a list of election fraud cases from across the country, broken down by state, where individuals were either convicted of vote fraud, or where a judge overturned the results of an election. This is not an exhaustive list but simply a sampling that demonstrates the many different ways in which fraud is committed. Preventing, deterring, and prosecuting such fraud is essential to protecting the integrity of our voting process."[53]   Fair enough, but if you're going to believe the Heritage statements, you really need to do due diligence. So I did, looking into their   database. I chose to look at Arizona, mainly because it came towards the beginning of a long list.

Roughly 2,300,000 people voted in the 2012 Presidential election. What I found was laughable. The following are representative of the roughly twenty examples of voter fraud.

> "David C. pleaded guilty to attempted duplicate voting during the 2012 general election. He received a fine of $4,575 and 117 hours of community service."

---

53 The Heritage Foundation. http://thf-legal.s3.amazonaws.com/ VoterFraudCases.pdf

"Regina B. pleaded guilty to voting twice in the same election, once in Arizona and once in Michigan. She was fined $9,150 and given 12 months' probation."

"Former candidate for Mohave County Sheriff Michael H. pleaded guilty to a charge of voter fraud for claiming on a voter registration form to be a resident of the county when he actually was not. Hays used a campaign worker's address in Mohave County when he filled out paperwork to run for sheriff."

"The M.s, residents of Green Valley, Arizona, admitted that they voted by mail in Kansas during the 2008 election--after they had become residents of Arizona. The couple also cast votes in Arizona during the same election. The pair pleaded guilty to a misdemeanor and were sentenced to a year of probation."

For Arizona, the Heritage Foundation database lists about 20 cases of voter fraud covering the years 2008-2012. Out of over two million people. As the Pro Football commentators are wont to say, "C'mon Man!" But how many people are going to look this stuff up? If you take what Heritage says without doing any checking, of course you can believe that voter fraud was rampant during the 2016 elections! But even their data show that their argument is, at best, deceptive. Believing that there are two sides to this story is a false equivalence.[54]

Or how about Darwin's "Theory" of Evolution (notice the quotes)? In the 2012 Presidential race, the human political lab rats of Iowa were polled about evolution. Only 35% of those polled believed in it![55]

What we have here is a difference in semantics. "Part of the problem is that the word 'theory' means something very different in lay language than it does in science: A scientific theory is an explanation of some aspect of the natural world that has been substantiated through repeated experiments or testing. But to the average Jane or Joe, a theory is just an idea that lives in someone's head, rather than an explanation rooted in experiment and testing."[56] In

---

[54] Postscript: "President Trump on Wednesday abruptly shut down a White House commission he had charged with investigating voter fraud, ending a brief quest for evidence of election theft that generated lawsuits, outrage and some scholarly testimony, but no real evidence that American elections are corrupt." Tackett, Michael & Wines, Michael. "Trump Disbands Commission on Voter Fraud." New York Times, Politics, 1/3/17. It is fairly obvious that if Trump thought the commission had a snowball's chance in hell of uncovering significant voter fraud that he would not have shut it down. The group owed its existence to Trump's inability to admit that he lied in the first place.

[55] Krugman, Paul. "Republicans Against Science." New York Times Op-Ed, 8/28/11.

[56] Ghose, Tia. "'Just a Theory': 7 Misused Science Words." Scientific American, 4/2/13.

other words, "In science, a theory is not a guess, not a hunch. It's a well-substantiated, well-supported, well-documented explanation for our observations."[57] After all, is the "theory of gravity" just a theory? If you're not sure, throw a ball up in the air a thousand times and see what happens. The two sides of this argument are not equivalent.

There's also another phenomenon... that of "truthiness." Coined by Stephen Colbert in 2005, and named Merriam-Webster's word of the year soon thereafter, "Truthiness is the belief or assertion that a particular statement is true based on the intuition or perceptions of some individual or individuals, without regard to evidence, logic, intellectual examination, or facts. Truthiness can range from ignorant assertions of falsehoods to deliberate duplicity or propaganda intended to sway opinions."[58]

A related term, "Proofiness," is the title of a 2010 book by Charles Seife which points out that numbers hold a particular ability to confuse and bamboozle most of us without a Ph.D. in math. Many of the claims made by politicians are positively "proofy."[59] Others who have posited that numbers can and have

---

[57] http://notjustatheory.com. Copyright 2007-2008.

[58] wikipedia.

[59] Seife, Charles. Proofiness: The Dark Arts of Mathematical Deception. 2010: Viking.

been used for political gain include Friedrich Hayek who used the term "scientism" in 1942 and Paul Romer with "mathiness" in 2015. Paul Krugman regularly rails against this practice, used by Republicans, to continue to push what he considers the false promises of trickle-down economics.

It is strongly believed that in order to have civil discourse about crucial issues in our society, we have to start with relatively similar beliefs in our echo chambers. And these beliefs have to be based in truth, not truthiness, and facts, not proofiness. Climate change is real and has a human component, evolution is more than a "theory," voter fraud is rare and tax cuts to the wealthy are not the best way to help the poor or middle class. Period!

It is tempting to wonder how so many people can believe and repeat such outrageous stories. In the examples above, it seems that someone with an axe to grind can say what they want because few people check to see if what they say is really true, or is a misrepresentation, a "truthy" statement, an exaggeration or just an outright lie. There is another explanation which will be roundly opposed by many… that is, that some people are just not that smart and are easily fooled or duped. On a statistical basis, half the people of any population, in this case our country, are *at or below average intelligence* as measured by tests that correlate with school performance. They can be excellent carpenters or car mechanics, or have "street smarts" but be unable to juggle complex social issues which require much reading, good verbal skills and a wide-ranging vocabulary. This will be discussed more at a later point in the book.

Donald Trump seems to be the king of truthiness. Has the reader ever, and I mean ever, met or known anyone who continually lies and engages in name calling and gives license to haters, and yet never admits to being mistaken? *Never!* Our president, by his refusal to admit wrong or apologize, must be the only perfect person on earth. Oops... I forgot a few other paragons...judged by the same standard Kim Jong Un and Vladmir Putin fall into the same category. Further, what should we call the people who accept or refuse to condemn those who pretend to be perfect? Sycophants? Enablers? Morons?

And although this book is not intended to carry a political message, there is one inescapable conclusion. There is an extremely high correlation between those that disbelieve science (climate change and evolution), that believe voter fraud is widespread (requiring strict voting laws), that giving tax breaks to the wealthy will (trickle down and) help the middle class and that will accept or condone base behavior on the part of those in power. These highly correlated beliefs are likely to cluster *primarily* in the echo chambers of very conservative Republicans.

Chapter 10: The Tyranny of the Minority

Political polls, for most of the time covering Trump's presidency (almost a year as of the end of 2017) place Trump's loyal following at around 35%. This cohort is loyal, stalwart and unbending. Their echo chambers contain beliefs that are rigidly pro-Trump. In effect, the echo chambers of Trump's followers contain, among others, many of the following beliefs, in no particular order:

> Finally we have a President we can understand; who doesn't talk over our heads and who gives us hope that things will get better.

> I like watching President Trump. He's funny and exciting to watch and I love when he is critical of all those double-talking politicians.

> Muslims must be kept out of our country, and watched within the country because many of them are terrorists and want to kill Americans.

> Many countries have taken advantage of us economically, preventing our economy from growing as it should and stealing jobs from Americans. We need to renegotiate our trade deals.

It is okay to think, talk and act in a hostile manner because we're just "telling it like it is" and there is too much political correctness out there.

The media are all biased against us. They make up fake stories to make us look bad.

They are all members of the intellectual elite who look down their noses at us.

We need to clean house, drain the swamp, because nothing Obama did has worked. We need to start over. Anyone who is "establishment" has to go.

Obama and the Clintons ruined this country and we have to take it back. Hillary and Bill are crooked and should be locked up.

We need to get rid of Obamacare and replace it with something better and cheaper. If Congress can't do it, let's do it by Presidential order.

Mexicans and other (Hispanic) immigrants will take jobs away from Americans. We have to get them out and keep them out.

Women can't take a joke. If a man comes on to them it should be flattering. And much of what we say is locker room talk. Sexual harassment is mostly political correctness.

Congress is totally ineffective. They can't get anything done so we have to work around them with Presidential orders or primary them.

The judicial system is too liberal and favors minorities.

Clean energy is anti-business. We need to bring coal jobs back and the EPA is a tool of liberals.

Democrats want to abolish the Second Amendment and take our guns away.

A summary of the above statements might include the descriptors paranoid, xenophobic, populist, fact-check-free and hostile. These are the new common beliefs that many Americans, most of them Trump supporters, have as a significant part of their echo chambers. These have replaced the old commonalities which included mom-and-apple-pie families, respect, civility and tolerance of differences. And polls showing loyalty to Trump indicate that this nexus of beliefs is relatively unchangeable. People have dug in.

How did these beliefs get into the echo chambers of Trump supporters? It is likely that it started in each person as some kind of dissatisfaction with something going on in their lives. Their job may have been insecure or they might have lost it. They may fear that foreigners will take their jobs at lower wages. They may feel as if bi-coastal intellectuals talk down to them or disrespect them. They might fear terrorism perpetrated by the "other." In effect, they see themselves as victims of something or another. And Trump, to his credit, found a way to make them feel as if he would solve their problems and quell their fears. He'll get them jobs, keep immigrants out and stop terrorists from coming to this country.

The immutability of his base was evident even before he was elected.

> "Even with his litany of disqualifying remarks, Trump's loyal followers are unwilling to hold him accountable for anything he says or does, no matter how outrageous or untrue. They are sending a message that they are sick of politics as usual and Trump is their populist conduit. But in that populist quest for retribution, Republican primary voters are investing in someone who represents everything they claim to despise—big-government intervention, fiscal irresponsibility, authoritarian tendencies, political hypocrisy, duplicitous tactics, and flat out

disregard for constitutional constraints. The contradiction is breath-taking."[60]

Our founding fathers were concerned about the possibility of "tyranny of the majority," through which the majority can place its own needs and wants above those of a minority (or minorities). This can lead to targeted oppression, persecution and despotism, brought about within and by the democratic process.[61]

There's also a related term, "tyranny of the minority," which is similar but implies that less than half the population can dominate the rest. In 2017, "the majority of voters who disapprove of Trump have little power to force Congress to curb him."[62] This situation obtains because Republicans have little desire to challenge Trump (who has autocratic and tyrannical tendencies), because they are afraid of losing their own jobs. Trump supporters generally come from red states and are very vocal, like their Tea Party ancestors.

In fact, Republicans have long used questionable but effective tactics to make sure that they don't lose

---

[60] Setmayer, Tara. "Donald Trump and the Tyranny of the Minority." Daily Beast, 4/4/16.

[61] wikipedia.

[62] Goldberg, Michelle. "Tyranny of the Minority." New York Times Op-Ed, 9/25/17.

the majority of seats in state legislatures. With almost unlimited money allowed in campaigns thanks to the Citizen's United Supreme Court decision, Republican PACs have carpet bombed state races with indecent amounts of money. They've also consistently tried to restrict voting by those who would almost certainly vote against them, meaning minorities.

> "Time and again, Republicans have cynically whipped up fake problems to justify real attacks on voting rights. They frequently claim to be working against voter fraud, which they paint as a huge problem undermining elections across the country. (In reality, voter fraud occurs at an insignificant rate in the United States.) They have used voter caging, in which a person's right to vote is challenged face-to-face, sometimes on the grounds that such voters no longer reside at the address where they are registered. They have instituted voter-I.D. laws, which penalize the poor, who are among the least likely to have state identification. And they have taken away the right to vote from more than 6 million Americans convicted of

felonies, a policy that disproportionately affects the poor and non-white."[63]

All this means that the roughly 35% of the population, whose echo chambers have been bought and paid for through what many think are underhanded methods, can run the show. And since the bases of these carved-in-stone echo chambers are lies, misrepresentations, exaggerations and deceptions, the fabric of American society is bound to change. The tactics used to capture the 35% make it very easy to see how autocratic and tyrannical regimes have ascended to power throughout the ages and, once ensconced, why it's very difficult to unseat them. No one gives up power willingly. As Mel Brooks said, in his 1981 film, "History of the World, Part I," "It's good to be the King!"

---

[63] Solnit, Rebecca. "Tyranny of the Minority." Harper's Magazine, March, 2017.

Chapter 11: Echo Chambers and Income Inequality

Let's consider the stability of a person's income. If I have a job and make enough money to put food on the table and a roof over my head I may be satisfied with the status quo. But what if my job or career is not going so well? What if my job has been displaced by robots, or has been outsourced to Vietnam, or the things I used to make are now imported from China? What if I'm still working but see my industry shrinking or about to disappear, as I might if I were on a GM assembly line, or if I were a taxi driver (replaceable by Uber drivers or autonomous cars), or if I worked in the printing industry (online news will replace me)? What if I am told, truthfully or not, that foreign workers, especially those from Mexico will soon take my job because they'll work for lower wages? What if I'm sixty years old and no one wants to hire me?

My echo chamber will have at or near its center, the belief that my whole way of life is in jeopardy. And I might be right. It's not *my* fault; I've done nothing differently or wrong. I badly need someone or something to blame. Or a group of people or many groups of people. And I need someone to give me hope. Enter Donald Trump. He tells me that Mexicans are taking my job; that he will bring jobs back to my industry (think coal); that the well-educated snobs and wealthy bankers that occupy the seats of power, especially on both coasts, are looking down on me and mine; that the media are part of that conspiracy to support the intelligentsia; that gang violence is the result of liberalism, etc.

Successful people, for the most part, are not likely to fall prey to Trump's messaging; in fact they are likely to look askance. They may go along with him as long as it makes them wealthier through for example, a rising stock market or tax reform. But their numbers are small. It is the much larger number of those people that are hurting, who are afraid the quality of their life will suffer, that will *enthusiastically* get on board. After all, they're down and really haven't much to lose.

Another correlating factor is education and/or intellectual curiosity. With education comes success, but also the ability to discern truth or at least question outlandish statements. If Trump avers that the ACA is "a disaster," or the New York Times is "failing," that climate change is a hoax or that other countries are "eating our lunch" does the person that hears these statements accept them blindly? I would argue that the more educated the person and the more that person is tuned in to *legitimate* news sources (which

Trump has tried to delegitimize) the more one will question those assertions.[64]

The result is that many people either don't examine the veracity of these claims or don't care if they are true or not. There are many that don't watch of listen to standard sources of news and get their information on Facebook. They want to "throw the bums out" and the ends justify the means. The current state of affairs is not working for many, and anything or anybody who promises hope and change will win them over. And unfortunately our form of government, it seems, instead of acting like a thermostat to wage inequality, creates a positive feedback loop[65] which tends to exacerbate differences in financial outcomes.

In a wonderful Op-Ed piece for the Times, Ganesh Sitaraman[66] points out that unlike Britain, whose system of government provides a

---

[64] Although I have not seen a study performed on this issue, I have noticed a huge difference in the vocabulary level between FOX and the two more liberal news networks. I would guess that the "delta" is around three grade levels.

[65] "Positive feedback loops enhance or amplify changes; this tends to move a system away from its equilibrium state and make it more unstable. Negative feedbacks tend to dampen or buffer changes; this tends to hold a system to some equilibrium state making it more stable." From: https://serc.carleton.edu/introgeo/models/loops.html.

[66] Sitaraman, Ganesh. "Our Constitution Wasn't Built for This." New York Times Op-Ed, 9/16/17.

counterbalance to class warfare, in the form of the House of Lords and House of Commons, our founding fathers did not preclude battles between the haves and the have-nots. Over time the rich, having more power, get richer and the poor get poorer. The resulting oligarchy in our country is what leaves us easy prey to a popular demagogue in the form of Donald Trump. And unless we can find a way to moderate income inequality, we may end up with a government that is more autocratic, such as Putin's Russia.

If there is no thermostat to dampen income inequality, the differences between the echo chambers of the haves and have nots can only grow commensurately. It's built into the system. If I have money, people are willing to lend more of it to me. If I don't, it is a lot harder to borrow. If I have good credit, the rate at which I can borrow is a lot lower than someone whose credit rating is worse. If I am very wealthy, I have quicker access to more information on which to base financial decisions. An insider will get shares of a hot IPO while a small investor will be denied. Only about 52% of Americans own stock in 2017[67] and about 63% of people own real estate.[68] Both

---

[67] "U.S. Stock Ownership Down Among All but Older, Higher-Income." Gallup News, 5/24/17.

[68] "What Percentage Of Americans Own Stocks Or Real Estate?" Financial Samurai Blog. https://www.financialsamurai.com/what-percentage-of-americans-own-stocks-or-real-estate/

of these figures are less than they were before the financial crisis of 2008, implying that many people could not benefit from the bull market which continues through 2017. If a person doesn't participate in the stock market or doesn't own their own home, how are they going to help finance a college education for their children or save for retirement or, for that matter be able to retire comfortably at some point? Again, the rich get richer…

Given that each one of us looks out for our own self-interest, a person who is struggling financially will resent and be jealous of those who have it easier. To rationalize his lack of success, he will denigrate intellectuals as being up in the clouds and not knowing what it's like to live in the "real world." If a "have" tells him to go back to school to learn a new trade or get a college degree, the have-not will justifiably say that he can't afford to do that and may silently believe that he's never liked or done well in school, so why bother? It's a lot easier to say than to do. All true.

A person that is comfortable financially will also look out for himself, so that he will rationalize away whatever guilt he may feel. He can call on other beliefs in his echo chamber, such as thinking that the have-nots are lazy or they don't work as hard as he does, that they have made poor choices in life, or they just aren't as talented. He deserves what he has and, obviously, those who haven't been successful only have themselves to blame. If have-nots show anger towards the haves, the latter will see it as sour grapes.

Income inequality is not new to our country or, for that matter, to the world as a whole. What is different now, as of 2018, is that the "have-nots" are more aware of their plight so that inequities can no longer be hidden or sugar-coated. It's one thing to be taken advantage of by the "haves," it's another to know it. And the single biggest reason for this knowledge is technology, in various forms.

As technology has accelerated, it has spread the pain across the lower end of the socio-economic spectrum. Joseph Schumpeter described "creative destruction" as the "process of industrial mutation that incessantly revolutionizes the economic structure from within, incessantly destroying the old one, incessantly creating a new one."[69] Creative destruction defines the loss of jobs and industries as society embraces autonomic vehicles, mechanized farming and the shift from print to online printing, among other fields.

And with the internet and social media, many people know, or certainly fear with good reason, that their lives will never be the same and that the outlook for their kids is bleak. If you are 50 and hanging on to your blue collar job in a manufacturing industry,

---

[69] Schumpeter, Joseph A. Capitalism, Socialism and Democracy. London: Routledge, 1942.

barely making ends meet, you can foresee the difficulty that awaits the next generation. It used to be that kids would follow their parents career, joining the assembly line or growing crops or working in the mines. All of these jobs are becoming scarce so that security is a thing of the past. There is not much to look forward to and the American Dream seems increasingly out of reach to more and more of the population.

So what are their options? Look for a "savior," a man like Donald Trump or Vladmir Putin, who promises to make their lives better, thus making them whole again? And/or bitterness and anger, which may lead to drug abuse, depression and violence? Revolution? It is no wonder that an increasing number of the intelligentsia fear for the future of democracy in general and America in particular.

> "It is not too much to say that a significant number of voters in both of America's major political parties see their adversaries as worthless. And history teaches us that the logic of worthlessness has chilling implications."[70]

The quote above is a reference is to Germany in the 1930s!

---

[70] Edsall, Thomas B. "What Motivates Voters More Than Loyalty? Loathing." New York Times Op-Ed, 3/1/18.

Chapter 12: Echo Chambers and Generation Gaps

    I recently read an interesting Op-Ed in the Times entitled "Stamped Out."[71] It was a lament about the not-so-gradual death of the hobby of philately, or stamp collecting. The author of that article has a collection that is almost worthless. Electronic mail and bill paying have largely precluded the need for postage stamps. Lifelong collectors are dying off, trying to sell their collections and young people don't seem to be attracted to the hobby. Thus while the supply of interesting and rare stamps has remained constant (being housed in collections), the demand for them has taken a nose dive and the bottom has fallen out of the market. The remaining collectors are at or close to retirement age, which implies that the hobby will continue to languish.

    No big deal, right? Who needs to collect pieces of paper with glue on the back? Well, I was one of those collectors. An avid one between the ages of 8 and 12, after which I would return to the hobby every once in a while. The time spent looking at catalogs of stamps for sale, at price guides and at my own collection, taught many of us youngsters a lot about the world and our nation, in a more palatable and

---

[71] Meyer, Eugene L. "Stamped Out." New York Times Op-Ed, 9/29/17.

indelible way than we learned it in school. "Before hours wasted on video games and other ephemeral pleasures, the hobby transfixed and transported youngsters. Stamps were the adhesive coins of the realm, a way to learn geography, history and politics."[72]

Time is zero sum, so what do today's young people spend their time doing instead? Gazing at screens of one size or another. I'm not quite sure what they are learning, aside from eye-hand coordination, but geography, history and politics are not on their radar. I'm not saying that what they learn from those screens is useless, or of less value than what I learned, but it sure is different.

Stamp collecting is just representative of the hobbies and interests that have given way to more modern ways of spending time. Kids spend less time outdoors, and more time in the world of game playing. Their interest in fiction comes as much from role playing games over the net as from books. They read less and seem to communicate more via a bunch of social network sites such as Facebook and Instagram. Virtual communication has to some degree replaced actual communication. And since the turnover in technology is accelerating, the gaps between generations are shrinking in terms of time just as they are increasing in terms of subject matter.

---

[72] ibid.

"A generation gap consists of the differences in opinions expressed by members of two different generations. More specifically, a generation gap can be used to describe the differences in actions, beliefs and tastes members of younger generations when compared to members of older generations regarding politics, values and other matters. While generation gaps have been prevalent throughout all periods of history, the breadth of differences of these gaps has widened in the 20th and 21st centuries."[73]

So, it is probable that the echo chambers of a 60 and 70 year old are more similar than the echo chambers between 40 and 30 year olds, which are, in turn, more similar to the echo chambers of 20 and 10 year olds. A concurrent trend is since people's exposure to music, data, information and biases are more and more unique, there is pressure on echo chambers to diverge even further. As things evolve, here are some predictions:

1) In 40 or 50 years, we humans may not need real people and real relationships as much as we do now. The more time we spend in virtual relationships, either through Facebook or similar online meet-up spots, the less time we have for actual people and the stronger our "relationships" become with people we've never met. We can be

73 "The Generation Gap." Investopedia. http://www.investopedia.com/terms/g/generation-gap.asp

quite "virtually social" playing multiplayer war games with people we call "friends," and fantasy football or baseball with "friends" that we love to compete with. There will be different rules for these virtual relationships than currently exist for actual relationships and the personal echo chambers of the future will be much different from the way they are today.

2) When families get together, parents often have to admonish their teens to put down their smart phones, while the teens would prefer to multitask, doing something on their smart phones and occasionally looking up to make or respond to a verbal comment to or from a family member. In the future all family members may be eating and conversing while *all of them* have one hand on their electronic device. If memory serves, when cell phones became all the rage over twenty years ago, people considered it rude if someone was overheard talking on their cell in public. Now it's commonplace and totally acceptable to most.

3) In the future, the people we confide in most may not be our actual "bffs," but those we speak to at a distance over an electronic device. It's easier if your confidant doesn't know people that you know and therefore can't possibly "spill the beans" on you. It's the same advantage that a psychotherapist enjoys today... when one knows that everything said will be

confidential, talking about intimate subjects is more comfortable and therefore likely. It is safer and easier to have intimacy at a distance.

4) Boredom may become a thing of the past. Even today, on public transportation people bury their faces in their screens. The same is true while waiting for a bus or a doctors appointment, or even going for a sit-down in the bathroom. With the ever-present smart phone, there is no need for "down time." Further, since what transpires on screens is highly motivating (think addictive games such as "Candy Crush" or "Farmville") it may be harder to get kids, or adults for that matter, to engage in physical and/or outdoor activities. We may get sedentary and fat. The addictive quality of the content on screens as well as boredom-avoidance may keep us increasingly yoked to those screens.

5) One may not have to have many common interests with the person you choose for a mate. It's okay if I listen to doo-wop and my mate listens to show music through our earbuds. Or if I play war games on my iPad while my spouse watches cooking shows. The most important issue may be that we both agree roughly how much time we spend on screens, regardless of what we're doing on them. If we are both okay with spending weekend nights in parallel but different screen activities, we might get along famously. Contrast this with the "Father Knows Best"

model, where everyone sits in the living room watching the same television program.

6) Needing to be less social, combined with the availability of information on line as well as the option to take more courses on line, may lead to less actual classes where people meet. It can be done virtually on the cheap, and if social connections are less desirable and require a commute, who needs a classroom? Or social interaction for that matter?

7) "The sociological theory of a generation gap first came to light in the 1960s, when the younger generation (later known as Baby Boomers) seemed to go against everything their parents had previously believed in terms of music, values, governmental and political views. Sociologists now refer to 'generation gap' as 'institutional age segregation.' Usually, when any of these age groups is engaged in its primary activity, the individual members are physically isolated from people of other generations, with little interaction across age barriers except at the nuclear family level."[74]

While it is common for children to think their parents are old-fashioned, it seems the isolation of the generations from each other has led to less knowledge of and respect for people who are older. The speed with which technology has advanced has not helped.

---

[74] wikipedia.

Older people have been left in the dust with the omnipresence of complex computers and smart phones. Even middle aged people are less interested in the latest tech, and thus become less able to keep up with the times.

This, in turn, has led to an increase in ageism, the discrimination against people who are older. Note that ageism is more rational with galloping technology. Would an employer rather hire someone who is facile with tech, or someone who has to struggle with it? And, incidentally, have to pay them more money because they have more experience?

8) Since technological advances seem to be accelerating (think "Moore's Law") will future generation gaps come more quickly as well? Driven by the self-interest of each individual, technology will doubtless make our experiences (and thus echo chambers) unique and will change the way we think about socializing and operating in relationships. Good? Bad? Who knows?

In conclusion, not only will echo chambers between and among individuals within each age group be increasingly dissimilar, they will be *more different* between generations and even members of the same family.

Chapter 13: Echo Chambers and Incivility

Politics have gotten increasingly polarized over the last few decades. In the interest of full disclosure, I usually vote Democrat in national elections, but I'm not blaming one political party or the other. There's plenty of blame to go around, and the march of technology, the disappearance of jobs caused by globalization, outsourcing of jobs to other countries and income inequality hasn't helped. But polarization can exist "the easy way" or "the hard way." We can peacefully coexist and agree to disagree, or throw verbal darts at one another and throw respect and comity to the winds.

Particularly insidious is the gradual march towards incivility, for which the poster child is Donald Trump. Many people disliked Bill Clinton, George W. Bush and Barack Obama, but the arguments were tame and the emotions controlled. By not having much of a filter, Trump has taken disagreement to a new level. Please note that I'm not talking about *what* he says, but the *way* he says it.

From the beginning of his campaign, Trump insulted just about all of his (serious) rivals in the debates and most of the cornerstone institutions of our nation including the courts, the Congress, the press and our intelligence services. Oh, and I forgot just about every minority group in the country and one of the two major genders extant. There are several negative consequences of this behavior.

The first is that because Trump is a combination of entertainer and boor, he has given permission to exhibit boorish behavior. Americans who have felt victimized by the system feel supported when Trump attacks that system. And gives them license to freely criticize it as well. No longer is it necessary to respect the feelings of others, so one can just say what one believes and call it "telling it like it is." Earlier it was pointed out that when people feel that their jobs have been eliminated through no fault of their own, they need someone to blame. Before Trump, political correctness precluded overt shows of hostility towards whatever scapegoat appeared. After Trump, why hold back? It's the Muslims, or Mexicans or the bankers or the intellectuals. Blaming someone for your plight is now okay, regardless of the veracity of the claim.

Changing course slightly, what happens when someone insults you? There will be a tendency to feel the insult as hurt, which most of us quickly convert to anger. It is much more acceptable to say, "I'm pissed at you" than to say, "that hurt." Admitting hurt makes us appear weak; showing anger is a (perhaps misguided) show of strength. The second thing that often happens is that we want to retaliate against the person who attacked us, with an insult of our own. Being insulted certainly doesn't make us feel warmth toward the person who attacked us. In fact, it is likely that we will dislike them and discount much of what they say. We will also think they are a jerk or an unmentionable male body part. That resentment, dislike or fear of the attacker will occupy a central place within our echo chamber. It will lead to ignoring or disputing anything that person says going forward.

As an example, if you are meeting a friend from work at a diner and he is 10 minutes late, you will forgive him and excuse his behavior if he just says, "Sorry." But contrast that with meeting a rival from work at that diner. If he is late, even if he says, "Sorry," you're likely to think he was rude and playing games. Depending on the relationship, we assume intentionality.

Trump, whenever someone is disloyal to him, or opposes him, or merely disagrees with him will attack, whether it is an individual, a group or a nation. Some people, those whose lives haven't been going well or those fed up with the inertia of the status quo, like this kind of outspokenness. Others hate it. In effect, he's really good at making both friends and enemies. Not just people who agree or disagree; people who either love or hate what he says. His behavior is divisive, and produces increased polarization between and among people.

What does this mean for echo chambers? First, it implies that there will be sharp divisions among and between the beliefs of the people of our country. Increased polarization, accompanied by a ramping up of emotional "skin in the game" will lead to stronger negative feelings toward people who don't agree with you. I would bet that anyone reading this book that feels very strongly either pro- or anti-Trump, thinks less of a person that they know from the "other side." How could they believe *that*?

The result is that tribalism increases, people retreat to their little corners of the world, voting is determined more by who you hate rather than who you admire, and that people who disagree with you are really bad people.

David Brooks discussed America after Trump:

"The best indicator we have so far is the example of Italy since the reign of Silvio Berlusconi. And the main lesson there is that once the norms of acceptable behavior are violated and once the institutions of government are weakened, it is very hard to re-establish them. Instead, you get this cycle of ever more extreme behavior, as politicians compete to be the most radical outsider. The political center collapses, the normal left/right political categories cease to apply and you see the rise of strange new political groups that are crazier than anything you could have imagined before."[75]

---

[75] Brooks, David. "The Chaos After Trump." NY Times Op-Ed, 3/5/18.

Chapter 14: Whose Echo Chamber is Correct?

It is clear that people with different echo chambers will see the world differently. They will accept and reject sources differently, and seek out and attend to different information. And because they start with different echo chambers, they will logically come to differing conclusions based on identical outside information.

Consider that witnesses to the same crime or accident often report different things. Or take horse racing. Bettors look at the same racing form ("pink sheet") and place their money on different horses. Note that this differs from opinions, such as I prefer the color blue or jazz music or Italian food, which come from within the person and thus doesn't require outside input. When outside input is involved, it is combined with preexisting constructs which comprise the nexus within an echo chamber to produce a conclusion. If I have a history of playing the ponies and think I know a good deal about the sport of Kings, then I read the pink sheet for a given race, and come up with a horse on which to bet, which is unlikely to be the same as the next guy's.

There's also an implication inherent in the existence of echo chambers that when people differ in their opinions, neither is right or wrong. How can that be? Well, suppose my wife and I disagree about whether or not to go out to dinner or to eat at home. I say I'd rather stay home and save the money, but she replies that if we stay home she has to do the work of cooking the meal. Who is right?

The answer is that we both are, for different reasons. From my perspective I'm right because saving money is good. On her side, she was tired and didn't feel like cooking. Both arguments hold water. *Both of us are right, but for different reasons.* Another difference is that we might both think that the other one started the argument. She felt that we had agreed to go out and by asking her to cook, I was trying to change the deal. I might have felt that going out was fine until she spent a bunch of money on clothes earlier this week, and that if she wanted to go out tonight she should've pushed those purchases off for a while. And obviously, we might both think that the argument started at a different time. I might've been upset since she came home with the clothes, and she got upset tonight when I asked her to cook.[76]

On a national political level, Andrew Sullivan makes these points elegantly:

> "Not all resistance to mass immigration or multiculturalism is mere racism or bigotry; and not every complaint about racism and

---

[76] Note that if we vary the wealth of the family being considered that one or the other might be perceived as right. If we are wealthy then saving money is less important, but if we are poor spending money on eating out is not such a great idea.

sexism is baseless. Many older white Americans are not so much full of hate as full of fear. Equally, many minorities and women face genuine blocks to their advancement because of subtle and unsubtle bias, and it is not mere victim-mongering. We also don't have to deny African-American agency in order to account for the historic patterns of injustice that still haunt an entire community. We need to recall that most immigrants are simply seeking a better life, but also that a country that cannot control its borders is not a country at all. We're rightly concerned that religious faith can easily lead to intolerance, but we needn't conclude that having faith is a pathology. We need not renounce our cosmopolitanism to reengage and respect those in rural America, and we don't have to abandon our patriotism to see that the urban mix is also integral to what it means to be an American today. The actual solutions to our problems are to be found in the current no-man's-land that lies between the two tribes. Reentering it with empiricism and moderation to find different compromises for different issues is the only way out of our increasingly dangerous impasse."[77]

A summary: When two people argue, they both think they are right, they are each talking about different things, they both think that the other started it, and both think it started at a different time. Relating this to echo chambers, both people come into the situation with different beliefs (premises/constructs) and when faced with the same event, which in the case above was "what are we doing for dinner?," each spouse logically came to different conclusions.

Note that this simple domestic argument is a paradigm for the differences between sects, nations and religions. The United States might blame Russia for invading Ukraine and Crimea as an act of aggression. Russia responds by saying that people in Crimea are native Russians and wanted to be annexed. Plus the West is posing a threat to Russia by putting missiles in Eastern Bloc countries.

Israel blames the Palestinians for violence committed against Jews and rockets aimed by Hezbollah or Hamas intended to create fear in Israeli's. Palestinians resent Jews for displacing them from land that they consider home and cutting them off from needed supplies and utilities. Shia blame Sunnis, Sunnis blame Shia.

---

[77] Sullivan, Andrew. op cit.
134

Without going into the details of each of these feuds, or taking sides, it's clear that different groups are certain that their dogma is right and the other guy's is wrong, and that if there is a conflict, the other guy started it. And each of the differing groups will be correct, but for different reasons.

Chapter 15: How are Echo Chambers Similar?

What beliefs or premises are central to almost everyone's echo chamber? To start, probably the ones taught by the world's major religions. The Ten Commandments tell us not to kill, steal, covet, commit adultery, etc. Most religions actively teach these principles, if in slightly different forms. Our parents, our places of worship and our schools instill common dos and don'ts as we grow up. Most are taught that it is not right to hurt the feelings of other people, that we should strive to act in a civil and respectful way. That we should only resort to violence in self-defense.

We are taught the Golden Rule, i.e., do unto others as you would have them do unto you, again, in one form or another. We are taught common courtesies such as saying please and thank you when making requests. We are told apocryphal stories of our heroes, such as little George Washington saying to his father, "I cannot tell a lie," after chopping down a cherry tree. We are taught that it is good to try to help people who have less than us, either by giving to charity or through volunteer work.

These rules that we all learn, and most of us follow most of the time, are the bases for similarities among all of our echo chambers. Remember that we are all motivated by feral self-interest. These common standards of decency act as curbs or limits on that self-interest. Without them, we might rape, pillage and murder, or at least be less civil and courteous to one another, and take advantage of people more than we do. The world would be a nastier, harsher place. As a perquisite, when we are civil and polite, we usually get more of what we want and our self-interest is served anyway. And even if we don't get more, knowing that we are acting well makes us feel better as a person[78] (which still serves our self-interest).

A somewhat disturbing trend has arisen with the phenomenon of Donald Trump. He was elected for a confluence of reasons, including his showmanship and charisma, which at the same time both thrilled and appalled different sets of people with vastly different echo chambers. His election victory seemed to be a reaction to politics as usual and the almost total ineffectiveness of the existing Congress. But in addition to his "throw the bums out" approach to campaigning, he may have changed the culture of our country by lowering standards for civility, political correctness, politeness, respect and empathy.

Every message contains two parts; *what* is said and *how* it is said, and the "how" has been changed drastically. Trump attacks individuals, derides political correctness, is intemperate and intolerant of dissent, plays fast and loose with the truth, displays misogyny regularly and winks at racial bigots. That is aside from any of the "what" of his views. Others

---

[78] This has been called "warm glow altruism."

have been able to support positions similar to what Trump espouses (end the ACA, strong military, strengthen our borders) without undermining civil discourse.

The result of the example set by Trump is that nastiness, disrespect and even violence may become accepted as part of many people's echo chambers. It is now more okay to more people to display bigotry, as in Charlottesville, to send hate mail to members of the press, to treat women as sex objects ("pussy grabbing"), and to shout "lock her up" at rallies. And while most of the recipients of Trump's direct or dog-whistle behaviors are now adults, younger people are watching. Will the next generation deride decency even more, having learned from their parents?

One has to wonder why so many people have either accepted Trump's behavior or chosen to turn the other cheek to his sometimes outrageous lies and attacks (again, aside from the "what" of his messages). The answer partly lies in the difference in the echo chambers between the haves and have-nots.

There may be a lesson to be learned, however. Recent events in the economic sphere (loss of job security, growing economic inequality), the political sphere (increasing tribalism and incivility) and even in technology (unique interests and experiences on screens) have made the echo chambers of Americans more dissimilar. The implication is that the way out of this problem is to somehow promote, develop and nurture commonalities in those echo chambers. More on this later.

Chapter 16: Echo Chambers and Psychotherapy

The concept of echo chambers, as used here, is the nexus (or system) of interlocking and interrelated beliefs, concepts, premises, values and attitudes which become increasingly fixed as we grow older. In effect, each of us is an echo chamber, and our echo chamber is us. The concept applies to everything we say, do and think. While the term has usually been used to explain political biases, it fits perfectly into the field of psychology and, in a concrete sense, into the practice of psychotherapy.

A person walks into a psychologist's office, having been brought up in a certain way. They only know what they know, which sounds obvious, but on second glance, is profound. Our echo chamber is the lens through which we see the world; we can know nothing else. As we grow, we will tend to cluster with people whose echo chambers are similar to ours. So in high school we will hang out with jocks or preppies or gearheads or stoners or nerds.

If we go to college we will be exposed, perhaps for the first time, to people with different views. If we don't go to college and go to work near where we were brought up, our friends and neighbors are likely to remain the same and our echo chambers will remain consistent with theirs.[79] One name for this tendency is "homophily," or "A theory in sociology that people tend to form connections with others who are similar to them in characteristics such as socioeconomic status, values, beliefs, or attitudes."[80]

A second term for this effect is "tribalism,"[81][82] wherein it's difficult to recognize cultural differences with other groups, since we only know what we know. We only hear opinions that more or less agree with ours, which reinforces those opinions and makes us more sure that we are correct and everyone else is wrong,

The person seeking help from a psychologist is likely to have portions of his/her echo chamber that aren't working well for him/her. She may tend to hang on to her insecurities, lousy relationships and self-defeating habits. A construct central to most of us is self-concept or self-image. If we don't like ourselves or don't think we measure up in any of a number of

---

[79] An argument can be made that people that don't go to college are likely to keep the same "people, places, things" in their lives and thus their echo chambers will not be exposed to differing views, compared to those who attend college.

[80] https://www.thefreedictionary.com/homophily

[81] Sullivan, Andrew. op cit.

[82] Ropeik, David. "How Tribalism Overrules Reason, and Makes Risky Times More Dangerous." BigThink, http://bigthink.com/risk-reason-and-reality/how-tribalism-overrules-reason-and-makes-risky-times-more-dangerous

ways (attractiveness, intelligence, achievement), it can lead to negative emotional states such as anxiety, depression or anger, which then lead a person into therapy.

Remember that an echo chamber acts as a filter, keeping out dissonant information, but also is an active seeker of consonant information. Thus if you tell a person who believes they are not attractive that they are indeed attractive, they are not likely to believe you. They'll just think you're being nice or polite or have an ulterior motive. And if a person who feels unlikeable goes to a party, they are likely to keep to themselves and stay on the periphery of conversations, with the result that (although others see them as reserved or unfriendly) they leave the party convinced that they are, indeed, unlikeable. These are the types of long and closely held beliefs about oneself that a psychologist must approach and, with the cooperation and assistance of the patient, help to change.

Even biologically driven behavior can lead to deeply entrenched maladaptive concepts that taint a person's echo chamber. Consider a youngster who has Attention Deficit Hyperactivity Disorder, or A.D.H.D. This is considered primarily biological, but the carry-on effects can adversely affect the self-image within the youngster's echo chamber. Left unmedicated, the youngster may get into trouble in school, perhaps be shunned by peers or (tacitly) disliked by teachers, have trouble paying attention and learning new material, and struggle to complete homework assignments. This may lead him to believe that he is not smart and is not liked by peers or teachers. At home, the child with A.D.H.D. may not be as obedient as his sibs, be "in trouble" more with mom and dad, and grow up thinking he is loved less. Though usually untrue, it does not bode well for his self-esteem. So while it is understandable for parents to be chary of medication, they need to accept the fact that there is a cost of *not* medicating that must be considered.

Echo chambers, guided by homophily, is another way to explain generation gaps. If teens only hang out with other teens, they will accept styles of dress, genres of music and codes of behavior that comes from within that group and, perhaps unfortunately, reject styles, music and behavior displayed and encouraged by members of their parents generation. Teenage oppositionalism is an outgrowth of this generation gap. Fueled by raging hormones, some teens will actively "feel their oats" and oppose anything their parents say or do.

A few other examples of echo chambers on display in human behavior involve the dating process. These days, many couples meet on internet dating sites. Those sites that emphasize what a person looks like can be deceptive, since attraction, though important, is only the first step to compatibility. One has to meet and get to know someone, meaning evaluate whether or not your two sets of beliefs that form your echo chambers are compatible. A site such as eHarmony, which makes the applicant fill out a long and arduous series of questions, gets to echo chamber compatibility much more quickly than a looks-based site. If eHarmony's algorithm predicts that your values, beliefs and attitudes are similar and you subsequently find a person attractive, the process may be much streamlined and less disappointing.

A person's echo chamber, hardened over time, can also be a stumbling block to re-coupling in middle age. Each person has his or her own baggage, which might involve kids, child support and alimony, ties to family, money or career problems and addictions. When older people meet, whether in person or on the net, they often see the good qualities of the other, and fill in the picture with what they want the other person to be, or hope he or she is. This can be called infatuation, which usually doesn't last. It is not uncommon, for example, for a couple to get along famously until one is introduced to the other's children, who take an immediate dislike to the interloper or the interloper finds those children disrespectful to both him and their mother. Or the couple gets along just fine until one discovers that the other has prodigious amounts of credit card debt, is hiding a serious drinking problem, or has ties to his former family that are too close for comfort.

A couple that gets married when young may "grow apart" if the man spends a lot of time out with his friends and playing sports while the woman takes care of the children and the house. After years of developing different echo chambers, the woman sees her husband as running away from household responsibilities and he sees her as a nag. He then avoids her criticism by avoiding her, and she becomes even more critical. They each have different values and interests in their echo chambers and neither is likely to have motivation to change. Not a great prescription for a healthy marriage.

A further roadblock for relationships formed in mid-life or later is that, after a time, we are who we are and like what we like, and see nothing wrong with that. Middle agers may be better off not re-coupling on a permanent basis. The woman is involved with her children and grandchildren, the man is less social and enjoys his time alone and playing an occasional round of golf. "Dating" may work better, spending time together on the weekends and living alone during the week. If they both accept this arrangement it may be the best of both worlds.

Each person can only control their own behavior. Trying to change someone else's is likely to be frustrating and come to naught. In the above example, the woman is not likely to get her companion to enjoy being more social or stop playing golf or bond with her grandchildren unless, of course, he wants to. And she is not likely to take up golf or give up time with her precious grandchildren. The best end state involves a lot of mutual acceptance.

The psychotherapist must try to get patients to recognize and understand their own echo chambers; what they contain and, secondarily, how they evolved. The therapist starts with the presenting problem, as explicated by the patient, and then helps ferret out the contents of the patient's echo chamber that are misguided, maladaptive or downright wrong. If the person is looking to find a compatible partner, their echo chamber may indicate the kind of person they will get along with best, or at least the kind of baggage in the other person that they can tolerate and what would drive them nuts.

People's beliefs are hard to change. The therapist can't control the patient, only influence her. Does she see you as a credible source, or as "fake news?" If the patient doesn't want to be there (as is the case with some teens dragged into therapy by their parents[83]) or the therapist is not credible, there is no way to even influence them. If a person is suffering, change may be hard to achieve because of the rigidity

---

[83] There is a small window of time, usually near the beginning of the first session, when the therapist must "strike while the iron is hot." Personally, this involves giving what the teen says equal weight to the parents' side of the story, taking the teen's side on some issue if at all possible, and using humor liberally.

of those (presumably) maladaptive beliefs. The rigidity that obtains within an echo chamber can affect, in similar ways, what happens in therapy and in the voting booth.

Chapter 17: Is There Anything We Can Do? Maybe? Please?

By far the solution most frequently proposed as a response to the existence of echo chambers and the gradual descent into tribalism is, "Listen to the other side." Right! Too little, too late for just about anybody who is tuned into politics and whose echo chamber rejects opposing views. People's echo chambers have been inoculated against opposing views, including a set of parallel rationalizing constructs, such as, for the gun issue, "it's a mental health issue" or "we need a good guy with a gun to get a bad guy with a gun." It's too easy to discount and deride the other side with well-practiced lines.

If one is serious about peeking behind enemy lines, it is suggested that the network espousing the values of the other side be watched *not just for an hour a day, or even a whole day, but for at least a week straight.* And give the experiment the same amount of time given to the news of the allies. If you watch Morning Joe (6-9 a.m.), Nicolle Wallace (4-5 p.m.) and Rachel Maddow (9-10 p.m.) every weekday on MSNBC, watch Fox & Friends, Neil Cavuto and Sean Hannity all of whom appear on FOX at the identical times. And, during that week, avoid any information coming in from the "good" side.

It is suspected that not many people will submit to the ordeal suggested above. And even if some do, their conclusion might be to just recognize that both sides are correct, but for different reasons. We need another strategy…

Another approach, obviously favored by Democrats, is to "throw the bums out." In the upcoming November 2018 elections, if the results are optimal for the Democrats the House, and perhaps the Senate, will tilt in their favor. With both houses of Congress, impeachment of President Trump is likely. Further, it will disempower the radical right and allow more moderate Republicans to step forward (instead of cowering for fear of being primaried). Both the catalyst for tribalism, our President, and his followers will be displaced by those wanting to restore civility and propriety. We the people have short memories and, within a year or so, it is likely that getting along will again be valued, and hating thy neighbor discredited. Not that lying and bigotry will disappear from society, but at least it won't be licensed and encouraged by the most important person in the country. Maybe the next generation will embrace comity.

Here's a pipe dream: There seems to be a whole host of men and women who identified as Republican or worked for Republican causes up through the 2016 election. Then they ran for the exits. The list includes Nicolle Wallace, Joe Scarborough, Michael Steele, Rick Tyler, Steve Schmidt, Susan Del Percio, Bill Kristol, Elise Jordan, Greta Van Susteren, Bret Stephens, David

Gergen, among many, many others. On the Republican side, there are two factions; the moderates and the ex-Tea Partiers, who now call themselves the Freedom Caucus.[84] On the Democrat side, there are the moderates and the further-left progressive wing of the party, represented by Bernie Sanders and Elizabeth Warren.

There have been times in recent memory when moderate Republicans and moderate Democrats have joined forces in an attempt to solve problems. A prime example is the "Gang of Eight" formed in 2013 by eight Senators[85] who devised and passed an immigration bill in 2013. It was not taken up by John Boehner's House of Representatives, but it provides a model of cooperative legislation.

What if centrists, i.e. moderates from both parties, formed a new political party. Call it the "America Club."[86] There are plenty of Republican legislators who can't stand the policies and tactics of

---

[84] About some of whom, Nicolle Wallace said, on January 25, 2018, "They've lost their minds, they're off the rails." Wallace served as White House Communications Director for President George W. Bush and was a senior advisor to the McCain-Palin campaign in 2008.

[85] Comprised of Republicans Jeff Flake, Lindsey Graham, John McCain and Marco Rubio, and Democrats Michael Bennett, Dick Durbin, Robert Menendez and Chuck Schumer.

[86] This name is appropriate because today's tribalism has put loyalty to party, religion, geographical location and skin color above loyalty to our country.

President Trump. Many of them are cowed by the threat of being "primaried" on the right by Steve Bannon-type candidates (although Roy Moore didn't fare so well), including the current Speaker of the House, Paul Ryan, who tiptoes around his responses to odious trumptrocities. As for Democrats, there are those who do not agree with the policies of the Progressive wing. What if they joined forces, perhaps in a Noah's Ark kind of way, i.e. two by two. Start with the gang of eight and recruit members from both parties. Joe Manchin, a Democrat and Jeff Flake, a Republican. Richard Burr (R) with Mark Warner (D). Susan Collins (R) with Sherrod Brown (D).

The Senate might be easy pickins'. The House somewhat more difficult, but if the 2018 midterm elections swing the House to Democrats, steam would be taken out of the far-right's sails. Membership initially would be by invitation only, until a majority of both houses are members of the "America Club." "Make America One Again" is a much more unifying slogan than "Make America Great Again." This author is not alone in fantasizing about a third party.[87]

Leaving grandiosity behind, the remained of this chapter will discuss universal approaches that counter tribalistic thought. The next chapter will suggest some specifics, many of which involve school curricula.

---

[87] Glover, Juleanna. "Are Republicans Ready to Join a Third Party?" New York Times Op-Ed, 1/29/18.

On October 30, 2017, John McCain gave a speech to the Midshipmen at the Naval Academy. He lamented, "We are asleep in our echo chambers, where our views are always affirmed and information that contradicts them is always fake. We are asleep in our polarized politics, which exaggerates our differences, looks for scapegoats instead of answers."[88]

McCain highlighted one of the main conclusions of this book...the more that our echo chambers differ, the more disagreement there will be between and among people. In effect, we are growing apart as Americans, as citizens of the world and as denizens of the earth. In America, it's not just Republicans vs. Democrats. It's white vs. brown, gay vs. straight, rich vs. poor, coasters vs. the midwesterners, America vs. China, believers in science vs. non-believers, facts vs. fake news. We are growing apart as a species, as if we were descending into an entropic state.[89]

It would be interesting to attempt to develop a measure of how much our echo chambers are diverging as a population over time. Put another way,

[88] Vazquez, Maegan. "McCain again takes on Trump, says 'it's time to wake up'." CNN Politics, 10/31/17. (http://www.cnn.com/2017/10/31/politics/john-mccain-naval-academy-speech/index.html)

[89] Entropy "...refers to the idea that everything in the universe eventually moves from order to disorder, and *entropy* is the measurement of that change." https://www.vocabulary.com/dictionary/entropy

how divisive is our society? One related measure already being used is called the "Gini Coefficient," named after the Italian social scientist Corrado Gini, who developed it way back in 1912. The Gini measures income inequality in any given nation or society. It is a statistic that measures dispersion and ranges from 0, which represents total income equality, to 1, which represents maximum inequality. In the U.S. as a whole, the coefficient is .469, the state with the most inequality is New York (.499) and, at the other end of the spectrum, the least inequality is found in Utah   (.419).[90] If some graduate student somewhere is interested, a measure of divergence/ concordance of opinions might add to the conversation.[91]

Further, the emotional volume has been turned way up, at least in part by the presidency of Donald Trump. Trump didn't start the rifts between the citizenry; the existence of those rifts helped to get him elected. The poor felt taken advantage of by the wealthy, whites felt encroached upon by brown people, the less educated felt looked down upon by the intelligentsia, and Main St. taken advantage of by Wall St. It's clear, however, that Trump's election has

---

[90] see Wikipedia: Gini Coefficient.

[91] There are other statistics which may be adapted to the purpose of measuring agreement among people. See: http://www.real-statistics.com/reliability/kendalls-w/

done nothing but exacerbate these trends. In effect, the information that comes from Trump World is both simple and direct. "Build a wall, tear up the Iran deal, tear up TPP, defeat ISIS, send troops to Niger and Afghanistan to kill terrorists, kill climate policy, kill family planning, cut taxes, raise military spending."[92] The problem is that for every person who loves what he says, there is at least one person who is reviled. Probably closer to two people.

Tim Cook, CEO of Apple, agreed. When asked about the influence of foreign (Russian) ads on our country, he averred, "I don't believe that the big issue are ads from a foreign government. I believe that's like .1 percent of the issue... The bigger issue is that some of these tools are used to divide people, to manipulate people, to get fake news to people in broad numbers, and so, to influence their thinking... And this, to me, is the No. 1 through 10 issue."[93]

A similar fear is expressed in a headline from FOX: "No, Russia didn't work to elect Trump -- It

[92] Friedman, Tom. "Trump, Niger and Connecting the Dots." New York Times Op-Ed, 11/1/17.

[93] Ortiz, Eric. "Apple's Tim Cook Says Dividing People a Greater Issue Than Russian Facebook Ads." NBC News, 11/1/17. https://www.nbcnews.com/tech/apple/apple-s-tim-cook-says-dividing-people-greater-issue-russian-n816536

works to divide Americans, with the help of Democrats."[94]

The divisiveness and tribalism have, in turn, amped up the emotional volume. Instead of Americans feeling pride in, and loyalty to, our country, despite differences, we now have factions, each of which sees itself as being victimized. We are told that America is being a sap for helping poorer nations and leading the civilized world, and a sucker for trade practices foisted on us by Mexico, China and other nations. Everyone is taking advantage of us, whether it is minorities, immigrants, other countries or the wealthy. Our judicial system is rotten, the media is biased, the intelligence services are tainted, Congress is ineffective. If all this were true, we should all jump off the bridge nearest our home.

So what, if anything, can be done about these growing rifts between and among members of our population? As a starting point, we need to be more aware of both the general biases of the sources of information on which we rely. "We need to know basic civics, our founding documents, how to think critically, and to distinguish the bogus from the truthful. We need social media to require truth in

---

[94] Hanson, Jim. Opinion, at http://www.foxnews.com/opinion/2018/01/28/no-russia-didnt-work-to-elect-trump-it-works-to-divide-americans-with-help-democrats.html

advertising, so that foreign adversaries can't stoke discord undetected."[95]

There is a website called mediabiasfact-check.com[96] that classifies major news sources into five major categories: left bias, left-center bias, least biased, right-center bias and right bias. They also have categories for pro-science, conspiracy pseudo-science and questionable sources. There are about 100 sources in each category. As expected, both MSNBC and CNN have a left bias and FOX and Breitbart have a right bias. NPR, the New York Times and the Washington Post have a left-center bias. The Wall Street Journal, Washington Times, New York Post and Forbes have a right-center bias. Those that are rated "least biased" include the Economist, the Congressional Budget Office, Doctors Without Borders, Reuters and Pew Research.

The same site lists the ten best fact checking websites.[97] All of them appear on the "least biased" lists. They recommend politifact.org, factcheck.org and OpenSecrets.org for political fact checking and snopes.com for checking urban legends. Those who want to be taken seriously in political discussions and

---

[95] Rice, Susan. "We Have Met the Enemy, and He Is Us." New York Times Op-Ed, 1/25/18.

[96] https://mediabiasfactcheck.com/2016/07/20/the-10-best-fact-checking-sites/

[97] https://mediabiasfactcheck.com/2016/07/20/the-10-best-fact-checking-sites/

anyone, teacher or parent, who is in the position of instructing youngsters about civics and our political system needs to be familiar with these sites.

There are also rubrics used at universities to vet information from the web. There is an amusing acronym, CRAAP, which can guide consumers of unverified information. "Thinking Critically about Web Information—Applying the CRAAP Test,"[98] where C stands for Currency (or Timeliness), R for Relevancy, A for Authority, A for Accuracy and P for Purpose. The test asks for ratings between 1 and 3 on each of the five dimensions, from which a total score of 0-15 is derived. If the score is between 12 and 15, the source is quite credible, if between 0 and 3 it is "CRAAP."

In addition to learning to do more "due diligence" it is believed that we need to better align the echo chambers of our population along certain dimensions. In effect we need to develop and teach a "common core" (although the term has been used before in a different context) of beliefs that we can agree on and live by. This common core should contain the following four broad categories: **Facts, Ethics and Morality, Respect for Expertise** and **Analytical Skills.**

[98] Blakeslee, Sarah. CRAAP test. Created at Meriam Library staff at California State University-Chico. Available at: https://www.csuchico.edu/lins/handouts/eval_websites.pdf

Facts: The first place we have to start is with facts. $1 + 1 = 2$, not 3. Up is up; it is not down. This is not negotiable. We can't permit people to think it's okay to not believe in things that are provable. Science is science, it is not smoke and mirrors. Evolution takes place, whether or not God exists. Climate change is occurring, and will change the way humans live over the next hundreds of years. Full stop. [99] [100]

Believing in, perhaps even worshipping facts may seem simplistic. But if someone denies them, what chance is there for reasonable conversation? You may as well try to have a discussion with a crazy person, one whose information comes from Martians beaming rays into his head. Discourse is not possible. But what if someone still thinks that Obama is a

---

[99] It is legitimate to argue that one doesn't care about the effects that climate change will have on humans; that we will learn to adapt since it is happening so gradually. But that is different from denying its existence. As far as whether or not truth resides in science, competition among scientists, peer review and replication of studies ensures that broadly accepted wisdom is pretty accurate. Not to mention a body of knowledge developed in many nations by many educated people over centuries. Science is not perfect, but it's damned close.

[100] There are times when you just have to shake your head, as when an Alabama politician tried to liken Roy Moore's abuse of a 14 year old girl to Joseph and Mary's parenting of Jesus. As Frank Bruni noted, "…logic and moral consistency aren't prevalent among Bible-thumping scolds." Bruni, Frank. "Jesus' Parents and Roy Moore's Gall." New York Times Op-Ed, 11/10/17.

Muslim, or Russia didn't try to interfere in our elections, or that climate change is a hoax perpetrated by China? Or any conspiracy theory that has either been disproven or has never been supported by facts, for that matter? What needs to be in the echo chambers of our population is both the desire and the ability to tell truth from fiction.

Questioning and doubting is fine, but believing outlandish stories despite, as examples, the presentation of Obama's birth certificate, the joint findings of 17 of our intelligence agencies, and the agreement of 99% of climate scientists is not. And if someone lies and/or shows ignorance repeatedly, how much stock should you put in his future pronouncements? And yet...

> "It is... difficult for most people to imagine believing that Hillary Clinton has had multiple people killed, that Obama is a secret Muslim who wasn't born in the US, that Trump had millions of votes stolen, that Barack Obama wiretapped Trump's White House, that Seth Rich (the mid-level Democratic staffer who was tragically murdered) was assassinated for stealing DNC emails and giving them to WikiLeaks, or that Antifa, the fringe anti-fascist movement, will begin going door-to-door,

killing white people, starting on November 4.

And yet millions of Americans fervently believe these things. Different polls find different things, and it's always difficult to distinguish what people really believe from what they say on surveys. But if 30 percent of America's 200 million registered voters are Republicans, and 40 percent of those don't believe Obama was born in the US, well, that's 24 million people, among them the most active participants in Republican politics."[101] [102]

Think about it… if someone believes in these conspiracies, what else must be going on inside their heads; their echo chambers? There has to be a supporting cast of beliefs that allow the person to rationalize away the truth and/or science and help

---

[101] Roberts, David. "America is facing an epistemic crisis." Vox, 11/2/17. (https://www.vox.com/policy-and-politics/2017/11/2/16588964/america-epistemic-crisis)

[102] A brief respite from the denial of facts that offers some hope is Mitch McConnell's statement, on November 13, 2017, that he "believes the women," when questioned about allegations against Judge Roy Moore. Previously, most Republicans would hedge their bets by saying something like, "if the allegations are proven, Moore should step down." After McConnell (and John McCain, who spoke up first) other Republican pols echoed the call for Moore to withdraw from the race.

prop up those false facts. Their whole network of beliefs is suspect, as is whatever comes out of their mouths.

A perfect example of this is looking at the people with whom Trump surrounded himself. Some have shady or radical pasts or reputations (Paul Manafort, Steve Bannon, Mike Flynn, Carter Page, Roger Steele, Alex Jones) and some were willing to sell their soul to the devil (Reince Priebus, Sean Spicer, KellyAnne Conway, Sarah Sanders, Jeff Sessions and a host of other sycophants who just happen to be cabinet members and/or spokespeople). Trump couldn't attract top flight personnel so he settled for what he could get... people with no experience, talent or ethics. Birds of a feather...

Timothy Egan wrote that the problem in our country is not meddling by the Russians...

> "... it's us. We're getting played because too many Americans are ill equipped to perform the basic functions of citizenship. If the point of the Russian campaign, aided domestically by right-wing media, was to get people to think there is no such thing as knowable truth, the bad guys have won.
>
> As we crossed the 300-day mark of Donald Trump's presidency on Thursday, fact-checkers noted that he has made more than 1,600 false or misleading claims.

Good God. At least five times a day, on average, this president says something that isn't true. We have a White House of lies because a huge percentage of the population can't tell fact from fiction.

Nearly one in three Americans cannot name a single branch of government. When NPR tweeted out sections of the Declaration of Independence last year, many people were outraged. They mistook Thomas Jefferson's fighting words for anti-Trump propaganda.

Fake news is a real thing produced by active disseminators of falsehoods. Trump uses the term to describe anything he doesn't like, a habit now picked up by political liars everywhere.

But Trump is a symptom; the breakdown in this democracy goes beyond the liar in chief. For that you have to blame all of us: we have allowed the educational system to become negligent in teaching the owner's manual of citizenship."[103]

Egan is basically arguing that much of the population is ill-equipped to tackle the task of citizenship and teaching more and better civics at

[103] Egan, Timothy. "We're With Stupid." New York Times Op-Ed, 11/17/17.

early ages will help. Although it is hard to disagree with his conclusion, ignorance of civics is just a drop in the bucket. More central is possessing the ability to discern fact from fiction when information coming at you is myriad and confusing.

Sometimes the truth of the matter is obfuscated by forensic tricks. For a lark, what follows is an article written by Gregg Jarrett and posted on the FOX News site.[104] My comments are in ALL CAPS.

> "Special Counsel Robert Mueller has sabotaged his own investigation of Russian meddling into the 2016 election. He has only himself to blame for ruining what could have been a credible probe.
>
> As I will document below, Mueller deliberately assembled a team of partisans with a history of political bias who appear determined to undo the results of the 2016 presidential election and drive President Trump from office." NO, HE DID NOT "ASSEMBLE A TEAM OF PARTISANS" AND YOU HAVE NO WAY OF KNOWING WHICH SIDE THEY FAVOR, IF ANY, WITH THE EXCEPTION OF

[104] Jarrett, Gregg. "Robert Mueller and his politically biased team of prosecutors need to go." Fox News, Politics, 12/9/17. At: http://www.foxnews.com/opinion/2017/12/08/gregg-jarrett-robert-mueller-and-his-politically-biased-team-prosecutors-need-to-go.html

STROZK. MANY OF HIS TEAM ARE AVOWED REPUBLICANS. PERHAPS YOU'D BE PLEASED IF EVERYONE ON HIS TEAM BELIEVED IN ALT-RIGHT CAUSES?

"…Because Mueller improperly stacked the deck of his special counsel staff with biased crusaders he transformed what was supposed to be an impartial investigation into an illegitimate and seemingly corrupt one." SAME ASSERTION. YOU ARE ASSUMING BIAS WITHOUT GIVING ANY EVIDENCE.

"…To restore integrity, Attorney General Jeff Sessions should un-recuse himself from the case for the limited purpose of cleaning up Mueller's mess." THIS IS THE SAME AS SAYING THAT THE ACA IS "A DISASTER." IT IS ONLY A DISASTER IF IT IS SABOTAGED BY REPUBLICAN LEGISLATIVE ACTIONS OR INACTIONS. ASSERTING THAT THE PROBE IS A "MESS" IS MAKING STUFF UP.

"There is no law that prevents the attorney general from doing this. Sessions should remove all of the partisans on the special counsel staff and replace Mueller with someone who can bring a measure of

neutrality and objectivity to the matter."
AGAIN, ASSERTING SOMETHING AND
THEN ASSUMING IT IS TRUE. THIS
ARGUMENT IS ACCUSATION-
INTENSIVE AND FACT-FREE.

"...Mueller also selected from the
ranks of the FBI an agent by the name of
Peter Strzok to serve as his top
investigator. Strzok has since been
exposed for his numerous
texts disparaging President Trump and
supporting Democratic presidential
candidate Hillary Clinton." YES. HE
SHOULD HAVE BEEN AND WAS
REMOVED. WHAT ELSE WOULD YOU
HAVE HAPPEN? PERHAPS HANG HIM?

"...Eight of the lawyers on the
special counsel staff are Democratic
donors." SO? HOW MANY GAVE TO
THE REPUBS? NOT THAT IT WOULD
MATTER. ARE YOU SAYING THAT
BECAUSE I GIVE TO ONE PARTY, I
CANNOT BE UNBIASED? DONALD
TRUMP GAVE TO DEMOCRATS.
PERHAPS YOU WOULD PREFER, TO
ASSURE NEUTRALITY, THAT ANYONE
WHO VOTED FOR, OR DONATED TO, A
REPUBLICAN OR A DEMOCRAT BE

BANNED FROM INVESTIGATIONS?
THAT WOULD WORK WELL!

"…It is no surprise that Mueller would be capable of unscrupulous maneuvers. After all, he maneuvered himself into the job of special counsel…" WHY? BECAUSE HE SERVED WITH HONOR IN THE MILITARY? BECAUSE HE WAS ESTEEMED BY BOTH REPUB AND DEM PREXYS?

"…Mueller had the audacity to accept his current position one day after being interviewed by President Trump for the job of replacing fired FBI Director James Comey. During the interview, Mueller never told Trump that he was considering investigating the very man who was sitting across from him posing questions. This was deceptive and dishonest." EXCUSE ME, BUT IF HE IS TO BE UNBIASED, SHOULD HE ALERT THE POSSIBLE, NOT CERTAIN, BUT POSSIBLE, OBJECT OF HIS INVESTIGATION? IS THIS IGNORANCE OR JUST STUPIDITY?

Garrett goes on to invoke the existence of a cabal involving Mueller, James Comey, Rod Rosenstein, Sally Yates and Andrew Weissmann, among others.

The logic is tortured and begins with the assumption that Mueller is biased and so everyone associated with him must be tainted. If one recalls, these are career public servants, most of whom served under both Republican and Democratic reigns. The conspiracy theory built and expanded by Jarrett is instructive however, in illustrating that if you grant someone's (in this case) untrue premises, how the conclusions drawn are valid, albeit untrue.

It is recognized that not everything is fact-based and often fact-based issues can be very subtle. Preferences are just opinions. But events that can be recorded either happened or they didn't. There is no wiggle room. And though, as with Rashomon[105], there is room for different views of the same event, the occurrence of the event should not be up for debate.

Ethics and Morality: Aside from facts, a second group of concepts/values that we need to have in everyone's echo chambers involve ethics and morality. A good place to start is with the teachings of the world's great religions which, give or take a bit, are more or less the same. They all teach that killing, stealing, adultery, being dishonest and coveting someone else's partner is bad. Although religions provide wonderful guidelines about how to lead a good and honest life,

---

[105] Rashomon is a Japanese film circa 1950, in which the story is told from the perspectives of a number of different people, who see things subjectively and thus differently.

and also provide comfort to people in their hours of need, rigid orthodoxy can and has led to strife and war.

The "organization" in "organized religion" leads to beautiful houses of worship and their accoutrements, but also provides a "brand" that must be defended and rationalized. Our religion must be better than theirs, else why wouldn't people desert our cause for theirs? Rituals, pomp, and individuals with careers to defend tell us why we're right and they're wrong. It might be better if all religion were personal; between an individual and their God, in effect, removing the middle men.

Another precept is the Golden Rule, i.e., "Do unto others as you would have them do unto you" or "Don't do unto others as you would not have them do unto you." It appears in just about every religion and is the basis for reciprocity, empathy, sympathy, altruism and social civility.

The need to focus on ethics and morality has been brought into focus by the phenomenon of Donald Trump. Just about all the existing norms for civility have been broken by Trump, his family and the birds of a feather he hangs around with. The insults have come so fast that people become desensitized and numb to them. It is hard to react to one slight, because the next attack or terrible statement will make it old news. Mainstream America is worried.

"I saw Ted Nugent, who on several occasions called for Barack Obama to be killed, grinning in a photograph taken in the Oval Office, or Kellyanne Conway appearing on television to urge America to buy Ivanka Trump merchandise. In this administration, crassness has become a weapon, annihilating social codes that once restrained political behavior, signaling that old standards no longer apply.

Lately, the pace of shocks has picked up, even if our capacity to process them has not. Trump's former campaign chairman has been indicted. One of his former foreign policy aides has pleaded guilty to lying to the F.B.I. about his attempts to collude with Russia. His commerce secretary, Wilbur Ross, turns out to have retained a stake in a company with business ties to the son-in-law of President Vladimir Putin of Russia.

The new head of the Environmental Protection Agency's Science Advisory Board once claimed that our air is 'too clean for optimum health.' USA Today recently reported that the president has nominated several members of his clubs to federal jobs. Never in modern history, it said, 'has a president awarded government posts to people who pay money to his own companies.' In another administration this would have been a major scandal. In this one it barely registers.

How can America ever return from this level of systematic derangement and corruption? I wish there was someone I could ask, but we know more about how countries slide into autocracy than how they might climb out of it. It's been a year, and sometimes I'm still poleaxed by grief at the destruction of our civic inheritance."[106]

Goldberg's comments imply that as long as Trump is President, it will be nigh on impossible for decency to be associated with the Oval Office. Trump's behavior is clearly unethical and immoral. Whether it is illegal or not remains to be seen.

Respect For Expertise: The third set of common core values should concern knowledge and talent, or expertise. I would love to know more about how my Honda works. But I don't and don't pretend to. The

---

[106] Goldberg, Michelle. "Anniversary of the Apocalypse." New York Times Op-Ed, 11/6/17.

way I look at it, if I had studied to be an electrician, plumber or carpenter, I might have been okay at it. If I had studied auto mechanics, I could probably fix my car. But I didn't and I can't. It's not that I'm dumb or can't learn, it's that I chose to focus on other things. I respect people who can fix things and use their services when necessary.

"…we've clearly entered a new age of politically potent anti-intellectualism. America built its world pre-eminence largely on the strength of its educational system. But according to Pew, 58 percent of Republicans now say that colleges and universities have a negative effect on the country, versus only 36 percent who see a positive effect.

And I don't believe for a minute that this turn against education is a reaction to political correctness. It's about the nasty habit scholarship has of telling you things you don't want to hear, like the fact that climate change is real.

Finally, we're now ruled by people who have no interest in letting hard thinking get in the way of whatever policies they want to follow.[107]

------

[107] Krugman, Paul. "On Feeling Thankful but Fearful." New York Times Op-Ed, 11/23/17.

Shouldn't respect for talent or knowledge go in all directions? There are many types of intelligence, among them musical-rhythmic, visual-spatial, verbal-linguistic, logical-mathematical and interpersonal[108], not all of which prepare a person to analyze complicated social issues. A person in a blue collar occupation might be quite "intelligent" but early on, for whatever reason, turned off to academics and chose the working class route. They often work with their hands and most still won't have much of an interest in academics now that they are established in their adult lives. To be frank, I don't believe that many of those people have the knowledge or interest in gaining the knowledge to understand complex societal issues (just as I have no interest in learning how to fix my Honda or my toilet malfunctions). Some will put in the time to read and learn, but most will not, and those that will not are easy prey for fake news, "shiny" news objects and made-up facts.

Although it may seem as if I am advocating a meritocratic society, where achievement, intelligence, education and experience, or some combination of the those, should determine who makes the decisions in the country, I'm not going that far. I do believe, however, that we need to put better tools in the echo chambers of everyone that gives them more ability to

---

[108] Gardner, Howard. Frames of Mind: The Theory of Multiple Intelligences. Basic Books, 1983.

tell truth from fiction and to analyze complex issues. Or at least, as Socrates is said to have preached, "know what you don't know."[109] It is hoped that the blue collar tradesman would know when he or she is out of their league in the same way that I feel inadequate staring at whatever is under the hood of my car or under my sink.

Because of the divisiveness in our country, it is easy for the hucksters and alt-right pundits to describe a narrative in which the bi-coastal liberals think they are "better than us" and look down at us. Therefore, we can't trust anything they say or even anything pushed by their "tools," the liberal media. And, of course, those media include the New York Times, the Washington Post, CNN and MSNBC. There is a strong parallel between those that work in the mainstream media and scientists.[110] As in science, there is competition between and among media outlets. If the Times gets something wrong, you can bet that people who work for the Post will be all too

---

[109] The actual phrase is more like, "The only thing I know, is that I know nothing," which has been called the Socratic Paradox.

[110] "Mainstream scientists and journalists see themselves as beholden to values and standards that transcend party or faction. They try to separate truth from tribal interests and have developed various guild rules and procedures to help do that. They see themselves as neutral arbiters, even if they do not always uphold that ideal in practice." From Roberts, David. "America is facing an epistemic crisis." Vox, 11/2/17. (https://www.vox.com/policy-and-politics/2017/11/2/16588964/america-epistemic-crisis)

eager to point it out.[111] What this competition ensures is not perfection, but relative accuracy. When a mistake is made in print, there is an effort to retract, amend or apologize. People who make really bad mistakes are brought to task and, if appropriate, fired.

In the words of the executive editor of the Pittsburgh Post-Gazette, "In the 15 years I have been executive editor, we have not knowingly published one story, or one paragraph, or one sentence, or one syllable that was not true. …The president's taunts have prompted long-overdue if uncomfortable and unwelcome reflection in our newsroom and others. But it has also prompted all of us to be more humble, more careful and more dedicated than ever to the basic elements of our craft: to marshal facts, produce stories and pay little mind to criticism, whether from left or right. To show, by our work, that the truth still matters."[112]

There is also competition between CNN and MSNBC with the same result of "keeping them honest," although the business model of TV networks lends itself to more impulsive reporting with less background fact checking. It comes as little surprise that the only competition FOX news network has to deal with are alt-right fonts of news. FOX caters

---

[111] Add the Chicago Tribune, the L.A. Times and Philadelphia Enquirer to this list.

[112] Shribman, David M. "Yes, the Truth Still Matters." New York Times Op-Ed, 12/11/17.

unabashedly to the right and there is no one on that side will question their slant on things or hold them accountable. In fact, FOX news, by picking up stories from alt-right sources and repeating them, serves as a megaphone for those sources. Without FOX, many alt-right sources would fade away. The goal of unbiased reporting might be better served if there were a second legitimate conservative news network.

Most know that what FOX broadcasts seems to show sycophantic loyalty to President Trump. Matthew Gertz recently pointed out that it's a two-way street, since Trump's early morning tweets appear to be regurgitations of the morning show "Fox & Friends."[113] Apparently Trump, a constant FOX hound, sees the scrawl on the bottom of the screen and within an hour or two, that content appears in his tweets.[114] This would be much less likely if there were a rival network that competed for conservative eyeballs.

There is one legitimate gripe against the elite and that involves Wall Street. In media and science the competition is structured to get at the truth, either in

---

[113] Gertz, Matthew. "I've Studied the Trump-Fox Feedback Loop for Months. It's Crazier Than You Think." politico.com, 1/5/18. At: https://www.politico.com/magazine/story/2018/01/05/trump-media-feedback-loop-216248

[114] A typical route for right-leaning "news" is for someone out to make money devises up a conspiracy theory, which is then picked up by an alt-right news source, which is then picked up and repeated on FOX, which is then heard and repeated by our President. Sad!

news or in research. Neither scientists nor journalists are in it strictly for the money. On Wall Street, the competition is for lucre; that's how success is measured. And unfortunately the money being competed for often comes from people who have less. The income inequality that exists today may be due in large part to the "haves" competing with the "have-nots" on an uneven playing field. And whether due to greater access to capital, lower borrowing rates, more timely knowledge or better connections, the "haves" almost always win.[115] Though our system of capitalism is defined by competition for wealth, it would help if the playing field were a bit more level. While we're all born equal many of us, by degrees, start with one foot in a bucket.

Analytical Skills: A fourth set of values or concepts that should be part of the common core of our echo chambers are a set of skills that allow us to discern truth from fiction, analyzing complex situations and methods of finding common ground (compromising).

---

[115] A reasonable analogy is offered by casino games. In roulette, over millions of spins, the house has roughly a 5% advantage. "Roulette is a drain on your wallet simply because the game doesn't pay what the bets are worth. With 38 numbers (1 to 36, plus 0 and 00), the true odds of hitting a single number on a straight-up bet are 37 to 1, but the house pays only 35 to 1 if you win! Ditto the payouts on the combination bets. This discrepancy is where the house gets its huge edge in roulette." Blackwood, Kevin & Rubin, Max. "Improving Your Odds At Roulette." Even at a slight disadvantage, repeated betting ensures that you will lose.

After all, the need to teach facts such as "Columbus discovered America in 1492" or to memorize state capitals is all but unnecessary today since the information is available with a few keystrokes. Instead, there is a need to teach youngsters how to filter, distill, process and digest information which is increasingly being "pushed" at them.

A real life example of the combination of dependence on facts, adherence to ethics and morality, respect for knowledge and talent, and possession of analytical skills is illustrated by a study by a group of researchers that examined the roots of gun violence in America.[116] The analyses performed were based on actual numbers, most of which were gathered by Adam Lankford, a Professor at the University of Alabama. The study deals with the ethics and morality that inhere to American society. These researchers have the knowledge and talent to perform complex analyses, and the skills to discern truth from fiction. What follows are the highlights of their report, of which there are many:

---

[116] Fisher, Max & Keller, Josh. "What Explains U.S. Mass Shootings? International Comparisons Suggest an Answer." New York Times, The Interpreter, 11/7/17. https://www.nytimes.com/2017/11/07/world/americas/mass-shootings-us-international.html?&hp&action=click&pgtype=Homepage&clickSource=g-artboard%20g-artboard-v3&module=b-lede-package-region&region=top-news&WT.nav=top-news&_r=0

A country's rate of gun ownership correlated with the odds it would experience a mass shooting. This conclusion was true when homicide rates were controlled, implying that it was not simply the level of violence in a society, but their access to guns.

Since the severity of mental disorders, the number of mental health professionals per capita and spending on mental health care is the same in the U.S. as it is in other affluent countries, mental health does not account for the difference in mass shootings.[117]

Countries with high rates of suicide have low rates of mass shootings, which would

[117] The idea that mental health professionals can pick out and/or predict those that will "go postal," as Nikolas Cruz did in Florida in February, 2018, is wishful thinking. "Mr. Cruz had suffered from depression and was getting counseling at one point. He was also evaluated by emergency mental health workers in 2016, but they decided not to hospitalize him. Why, some critics are demanding, didn't he receive proper treatment? And can't we just stop angry, unstable young men like him from buying firearms? It's much harder than it sounds. The mental health system doesn't identify most of these people because they don't come in to get care. And even if they do, laws designed to preserve the civil liberties of people with mental illness place limits on what treatments can be imposed against a person's will." Barnhorst, Amy. "The Mental Health System Can't Stop Mass Shooters." New York Times Op-Ed, 2/20/2018.

not be the case if mental health were involved.

Americans are no more likely than citizens of other developed countries to play video games which rules out their relationship to mass shootings.

Racial diversity and immigration (in Europe) show little correlation with either gun murders or mass shootings.

America is a violent country. The homicide rate here was 33 per million in 2009, compared to Canada (5 per million) and Britain (.7 per million), which corresponds to the difference in number of guns owned.

The U.S. does not have higher rates of crime than other developed countries, but when a crime does occur, on average it is more lethal (from Franklin E. Zimring and Gordon Hawkins, U. California at Berkeley). For example, a New Yorker is just as likely to be robbed as someone from London, but is roughly 50 times more likely to be killed in the robbery.

Gun related deaths in the U.S in 2013 included over 21,000 suicides, over 11,000 homicides and over 500 death by accidental discharge of a gun. By comparison Japan, which has one-third of our population, had 13 deaths in the same time period. Thus an American is 300 times more likely to die from being shot than someone in Japan.

Among all the variables examined by this study and all others referenced, the only one that mattered was the number of guns owned in a given country. This held across developed countries, among American states, when controlled for crime rates and mental health problems. And gun control legislation reduced gun murders in 130 studies performed in 10 countries.

If people want to argue that the burgeoning number of gun deaths is a cost that we are willing to pay to protect our right to bear arms, that's okay… that's a value judgment. But the data presented by this and other studies are factual and not fake news… full stop.

Adding to the conclusions from the above…Our founding fathers unintentionally screwed us by writing the Second Amendment the way they did. It reads, "A well regulated militia being necessary to the security of a free state, the right of the people to keep and bear arms shall not be infringed." Changing a few words, such as the addition of "in times of war" at the end would've saved thousands of lives over the years. The founders could not have anticipated the burgeoning number of guns, the much greater killing power, range and rapidity of fire. Seemingly no other country wrote their version of our Constitution that way. Part of the problem is that we came into being fairly late in the game and violence was built into our social mores.

Using a baseball analogy, if a .300 batter gets up 100 times, he is likely to get 30 hits. If he gets up 10 times, he is likely to get 10 hits. If a hundred million people have guns and the likelihood that a person will shoot someone else is one in a million (in a year), one would expect that 100 people would get shot. If there are 10 million guns, the expectation drops to ten people being shot.

Another factor is how many rounds a gun can hold. If the maximum available number of rounds per gun were to be three, fewer people would die when guns are used than if the maximum number of rounds is 30.

If someone is barred from buying or owning a gun if found to be involved in domestic violence, what happens if they buy a gun in the years before domestic violence occurs? Do the police ensure that perpetrators of domestic violence turn in guns that they may own, or confiscate the ones stored in their basement?

There is no question that a person has to be "mentally ill" or "crazy" or "having a breakdown" in order to shoot someone other than in self-defense. But most people aren't crazy all the time. A person can lead a normal life, own guns for years and "flip out" when they are in their 50s. Then they kill someone. And predicting who will "go off the deep end" or when they will do so, is not even remotely possible. It's similar to the baseball analogy. The more guns extant in a society, given a constant rate of people "going crazy," the more people will get shot.

The upshot is, that we are basically out of luck as a society. It does little good to close the barn door after the horses have escaped. Ideally, we would stop the manufacture and sale of guns from now on, offer stipends to people to turn in their guns, ban auto- or semi-automatic weapons, and limit the number of rounds in a gun. Unfortunately, none of this will happen.[118] Which only proves the power of "emotional thinking" (an oxymoron) to ignore logical processes.

---

[118] The Parkland school shooting in Florida, which aroused young people to protest and retired Justice John Paul Stevens' Op-Ed calling for the repeal of the Second Amendment holds out hope, but there is still a long way to go.

Chapter 18: Some Specific Ideas Concerning Echo Chambers

First, it is recognized that most of what will be discussed will take years to establish, take root and counter the prevailing trends. Education of youngsters is the place to start, and the earlier the better. Some religions (orthodoxies) and countries (North Korea) start thorough indoctrination early which makes later changes to a person's echo chamber unlikely. Changes in emphasis in an American child's education might include:

1) **Teach less factual information** in the realm of social studies to provide more time to teach conceptual views of civics, current events and history. This author can recall learning about and having to memorize facts (names and dates) about the Civil War and the battles that comprised it, which only served to bore me, lead to disinterest and studying only to the test. After the test, all was forgotten. Looking back, spending more time on the predecessors and causes of the Civil War would have created a longer lasting impression and made more sense and, en passant, made the subject much more attractive. If at some later point in time details about time, place and person become of interest, answers are a few clicks away. And if the knowledge base of the general situation of the times and the causality of events were in a person's echo chamber, this would provide a

"skeleton" on which those specific facts could adhere to.

2) **Emphasizing fiction less and non-fiction more**. When we are young, fiction in the form of fairy tales does help us learn right from wrong, ethical behavior and other general values. As we get older, however, it is not clear that what we learn from fiction is valuable, at least per unit of time spent. "Happily ever after" novels or lengthy series of detective books teach lessons with a rapidly decreasing rate of return. One or two of each may be enough. And although Steven King's type of horror stories, fantasy series or zombie apocalypse books do hold one's interest,[119] they don't quite help develop a good picture of what the real world is like. In fact, if the fiction we read is only superficially attached to reality, it may very well make us more susceptible to and accepting of conspiracy theories later in life. If we believe that anything is possible as a child or teen, we may tend to feel more that way as adults. After all, Elvis lives, doesn't he?

3) **Emphasize mathematical thought and deemphasize memorizing math facts.** Everyone used to be taught and made to memorize the four basic math operations, at least for smaller numbers. Almost every adult that I know, with the exception of a few

---

[119] As do video games…

engineers (who live with math-related subjects throughout their careers), can't do anything but the simplest problems in their head, such as figuring how much a discount will save you or how much to leave for a 15% tip. There are several reasons. One, just like any other set of facts, including Civil War battles, if you don't use it, you lose it. Most people don't use math in their careers or lives and just don't have a reason to retain arcane facts. Second, almost everyone has a calculator on their cell phones and even before those were everywhere, many people depended on hand held or desk calculators. (Even my accountant does…)

Third, stores and advertisers do the numbers for us. In supermarkets, there are tags above or below each item, stating not only the price, but the price per unit. Department stores often advertise "10% off with coupon" or "take an additional 15% off anything in the store." My wife, a very bright woman, will often come home and say something like, "It was already marked 30% off, and they were giving an additional 15% discount!" Now the first thing is, those "disclosures" make us lazy and not interested in doing the numbers ourselves, and second, we have no way of knowing whether the item purchased was a bargain or a rip off. I don't know anyone who, under those conditions, will do the due diligence.

Last, online marketplaces such as Amazon make mental price comparisons unnecessary. If I put, "#3 blue automatic widget" into their search engine, Amazon will return all of the products that fit into that description, with prices and shipping costs attached and added for me. Why would I have to know math facts at all?

Instead, emphasis needs to be placed on "thinking mathematically." I need to understand the relationship between length, area and volume, I don't have to know how to calculate volume. I need to know how the radius, circumference and area of a circle relate to one another, I don't need to know how to calculate them. Learning how to estimate may be more important than learning how to calculate.

4) **Teach logical processes, including deductive and inductive logic and logical fallacies.** "…in a deductive argument, the premises are intended to provide such strong support for the conclusion that, if the premises are true, then it would be impossible for the conclusion to be false."[120] "An inductive argument is an argument that is intended by the arguer to be strong enough that, if the premises were to be true, then it would be *unlikely* that the conclusion is false. So, an inductive argument's success or strength is a matter of degree, unlike with deductive arguments."[121]

---

[120] Internet Encyclopedia of Philosophy: a Peer-Reviewed Academic Resource. At: http://www.iep.utm.edu/ded-ind/

[121] ibid.

Deduction is considered a top-down process, so that one starts with the general and ends up with the specific. Induction starts with a specific observation and ends up with a general conclusion.

Once the basics of deduction and induction are understood, discussion of logical fallacies is both interesting and helpful to thinking through problems that adults face in a complex world. It will hone the ability of people to discern truth from fiction.

For example, the "Strawman" fallacy involves making up or exaggerating someone's point of view to make your own argument sound more reasonable. For instance, "After Will said that we should put more money into health and education, Warren responded by saying that he was surprised that Will hates our country so much that he wants to leave it defenseless by cutting military spending."[122] If people can't see that Warren's response is a lie and irrelevant to the issue, they will be easy prey for hyperbolic political arguments. Not just as regards politics, but in their own adult relationships. If your boyfriend asserts, "you'd rather spend time with your friends than with me," an appropriate response might be, "They are not mutually exclusive."

Correlation and Causation are easily confused. "Pointing to a fancy chart, Roger shows how temperatures have been rising over the past few

[122] "Your Logical Fallacy Is" at https://yourlogicalfallacyis.com/strawman

centuries, whilst at the same time the numbers of pirates have been decreasing; thus pirates cool the world and global warming is a hoax."[123] Because two things occur simultaneously in time does not mean that "a" caused "b," or "b" caused "a" or that there is any relationship at all between them. Note how President Trump claims credit for anything good that happens and denies responsibility for anything bad, but there is no indication that causality is operating. His claims could be wholly true, totally false or anywhere in between. There is not enough information to make that call. A response might be, "Show me how those things are related."

Or the "Slippery Slope" argument. This is the favorite of the N.R.A., which argues that if we allow the banning of bump stocks (which allow conversion of semi-automatic weapons to automatic ones), or make background checks for firearms more rigorous or ban domestic abusers from buying guns, that pretty soon "they'll be coming for our guns." This, in effect, changes the subject totally and tries to equate extreme hypothetical cases with everyday ones. "…if we allow same-sex couples to marry, then the next thing we know we'll be allowing people to marry their parents, their cars and even monkeys."[124]

And then there's always the "ad hominem"

---

[123] ibid.

[124] ibid.

argument in which instead of rebutting someone's assertion, you attack their character with the intention of negating whatever they say and changing the subject.

Logic, along with logical fallacies, are essential to know and understand if we are to be able to tell fact from fiction. If Labron James wants to teach me something about basketball, I'm all ears, but if he's trying to sell me a car or a phone service, I consider everything he says irrelevant. He has no more expertise in those areas than I have. But it started a lot earlier than Labron. Does anyone remember "Tony the Tiger" pushing Kellogg's Frosted Flakes? Tony, as is Labron, is *irrelevant* to the quality or value of the product. In fact "irrelevant" may be one of the most important words in the English language and the earlier we understand it and can use it properly, the better off we will be.

4) **Teach Skills for Truth-telling.** Several BBC journalists are attempting to develop programs to enable children to tell real news from fake news. They are aiming to provide 1000 schools in Britain with online and in-class help beginning in March 2018.[125] These kinds of efforts are wanted and needed, but it is likely that efforts will have to begin early in the

[125] "BBC to help students identify 'fake news'." BBC News, 12/6/17. At: http://www.bbc.com/news/entertainment-arts-42242630

education process and continue throughout the school years.

> "...educators must help turn students into educated voters. Too many schools fail to provide students with tools of logic that would enable them to assess the quality of information they absorb from every screen. All schools, for example, should have a curriculum that teaches children how to evaluate online information."[126]

There are some basic protocols that can be built into school curricula. A child with a computer can learn how to fact check at an early age. If one puts a current event into a search engine, many responses will be returned. Scanning them may reveal whether they come from legitimate sources and general agreement among them or, to the contrary, seemingly arcane sources that are "one offs." If a story from one of these odd sources contains even a modicum truth, the legitimate news sources will check them out and expand upon them.[127]

News obtained from any social network source, where stories are repeated or retweeted by

---

[126] Jacoby, Susan. "Stop Apologizing for Being Elite." New York Times Op-Ed, 3/16/18.

[127] Learning about and utilizing sites that evaluate media sources for bias, such as mediabiasfactcheck.com will certainly help.

nonprofessionals should *never* be trusted unless echoed by, or traceable to, major legitimate news sources (and not taken out of context). Part of teaching youngsters to avoid news from social networks is to examine the motivations and agendas of those pushing the news. There will almost always be a secret agenda, whether it has a political purpose or just an attempt to sell corn flakes.

5) **Teach age appropriate statistics concepts early.** While it may not be essential for everyone to be able to calculate statistics, understanding them conceptually is paramount. This is especially necessary to understand conclusions based on inductive reasoning. If I say that ninety-nine percent of scientists agree that humans contribute to global warming with a high degree of confidence, it would be hoped that everyone would understand that this is more than "just a theory."

If one understands a little bit of statistics, such as sample size, then it is possible to realize that when someone says, "I am doing worse under the ACA" or "some people are saying…," that this is a very small sample size, perhaps even a sample size of one. And thus is meaningless when trying to make an assertion. A person's story might be the exception, the rule, or somewhere in between. In order to know this, we have to know how many people were queried randomly[128] and how many feel they are suffering or benefitting. Otherwise what is being offered is "anecdotal evidence," which is another logical fallacy. And we also have to consider the possibility that the story was totally fabricated.

> "President Trump claims personal knowledge of the undeserving poor. 'I know people that work three jobs and they live next to somebody who doesn't work at all,' he said in Missouri last month. The sponger 'is making more money and doing better than the person that's working his ass off.' Wow. Sounds awful. And almost certainly not true. Trump did not cite the source of his tale of two households. And it's doubtful, in the friendless circle of clueless rich people with whom he shares Diet Cokes, that he actually 'knows people' living next to welfare bums."[129]

Statistical concepts such as the bell curve (normal curve), random sampling, sample size, standard deviation (and variance) as well as measures

---

[128] And to understand the meaning of *random* sampling.

[129] Egan, Timothy. "The Deserving Rich and the Deserving Poor." New York Times Op-Ed, 12/15/17.

of central tendency are essential to understanding numerical statements pushed at you.

6) **Teach scientific method and experimentation** including the steps of making observations, developing hypotheses to examine the cause of what was observed, making predictions about what will occur if the hypothesis is true or not, developing a procedure to gather data to test the hypothesis, tabulating the results of the experiment and analyzing those results to reach conclusions about the truth or falsity of your hypothesis.[130] Children can master this at an early age and will gain confidence in their own ability to come to logical conclusions. It may also help to foster a respect for scientific evidence when they get older.

7) **Teach the meaning of "enabling."** Adults should be able to discern when some people, by their silence and/or inaction, allow others to continue to behave badly (think the "me-too" movement and the silence of many Republicans about Roy Moore). For youngsters, an example might be laughing at a classmate who is trying to get attention by acting out. Or not saying something if a classmate steals another one's pencil. Although bullying in school has received much attention lately, classmates who keep silent

---

[130] Khan Academy. At: https://www.khanacademy.org/science/biology/intro-to-biology/science-of-biology/a/the-science-of-biology

when they see bullying need to be taught to speak up. Speaking up when young will make it easier to do so when an adult. Every person is responsible for their own actions (and inactions) so that if you don't say anything and enable, you too are culpable.

8) **Teach methods of compromise.** If we can accept that we are not always right or, that both you and the other person are both right for different reasons, and that we don't always have to win, then we can look to compromise to come up with a resolution acceptable to both parties. Here are four ways of compromising:

a) **Averaging**: Some disagreements occur on variables, such as time and money, which can be scaled, and thus averaged. If one spouse wants to spend $2000 on this year's family vacation and the other spouse thinks the family can only afford $1000, then $1500 would be a compromise. If one friend wants to meet at 7:00 p.m. and the other at 8:00 p.m., a solution is to meet at 7:30 p.m. Note that the arrived-at number does not have to lie directly in the middle. If one friend cannot get out of work early, the meeting time could be set at 7:45 p.m. Though not in the middle, it does concede something to both participants in the disagreement. This makes for good will, allows both sides to "save face" and discomfits and benefits both sides.   In a wider arena, if the leaders of one major particular party wants to dedicate x billion dollars to a particular national program, and the leaders of the other major party want to spend y billions, numbers between x and y represent compromises. Often the U.S. Senate and House of Representatives craft and pass similar bills that differ in the amount of funding, and that the two versions need to be aligned so that the bill will pass.[131]

b) **Veto Power**: Generally, if I like choice A and you prefer B, we decide to have reciprocal veto power over each other's choices and must look for C, a choice we both can live with. A husband likes Colonial furniture, his wife likes Danish Modern. Each vetoes the other's first choice and they must look for a third style that they both agree on, say French Provincial. One spouse wants a four-door sports car, the other wants a minivan for the family. The compromise might be, after cross-vetoes, a "crossover" vehicle or

---

[131] The process even has a name… "reconciliation."

station wagon. Or you dislike Mexican food, I hate Chinese food, so we eat Italian or at a burger joint, or at a diner where each of us can find something we like.

Veto power is an integral part of the negotiating process at the United Nations. Members of the Security Council may veto each others declarations, usually based on political beliefs. Knowing that a proposed declaration faces possible veto leads to interesting posturing. A country may propose something to make a point even knowing that it will be vetoed, or the language of a proposal may be nuanced in such a manner meant to avoid a veto or reduce controversy.

In the United States, the President has veto power over bills passed by Congress and presented to him. Conversely, Congress can "veto the veto" by overriding the President's veto with a two-thirds vote by both Houses of Congress.

c) **Alternation of realms**: Both parties trade off so that each has a constant area of control. One spouse dislikes yard work while the other hates doing the laundry. The yard-hater does the laundry and the laundry-hater tends to the yard. Or one does the "inside work" while the other takes care of anything outside. Or one takes the responsibility of arranging social plans with friends and family, while the other takes care of the finances (paying bills, investing, budgeting). That's not to say that the social director should not have input to financial decisions or the accountant can't express preferences for who the couple sees on Saturday night, but each realm has a "Captain" or leader.

Most governments divide power. In the U.S. we have three branches of government, each with its own purview. The President assigns cabinet positions, in effect, defining areas of turf for the various appointees. The CIA has its portfolio, as does the Department of Interior, State, Treasury, etc. Other countries have their own territorial arrangements (e.g. Great Britain has the House of Lords, the House of Commons, M.I.5, etc.)

d) **Alternation of choices within realms**: I like Mexican food, you like Chinese food. We alternate choices, so that this week the choice is mine, next week yours. Same with movies, either in theaters or with rentals.

One week it's Clint Eastwood, the next it's Meryl Streep. If one of us tends to always pick movies that the other can't abide, such as violent films, we may be better off with strategy b) above, where we both have a veto.

At the United Nations, smaller nations take turns sitting on the Security Council. The sites for both Winter and Summer Olympics rotate between countries, as do the sites for other international meetings. Countries that can play nicely together by taking turns are seen as cooperative.

All four of these strategies, if used, leave the participants feeling good (or less bad) about each other and feeling as though they make a good "team." Each also saves face, if the results of the compromise are visible to others. Both sides get something, though not all of what they want. And a successful compromise sets a good precedent for future situations where the parties disagree.

9) **Increase pressure on social network companies** to change their policies and police their sites. Many of us have taken "personality tests" online. They commonly produce an "OCEAN score," so named because we are rated on five dimensions: Openness, Conscientiousness, Extraversion,

Agreeableness and Neuroticism. This score, though seemingly innocent, can and has been used to nefarious ends. There's a company called Cambridge Analytica, which has used data collected from and about us on Facebook for political purposes.[132] More specifically, the data was used by the campaign to elect Donald Trump.

> "One recent advertising product on Facebook is the so-called "dark post": A newsfeed message seen by no one aside from the users being targeted. With the help of Cambridge Analytica, Mr. Trump's digital team used dark posts to serve different ads to different potential voters, aiming to push the exact right buttons for the exact right people at the exact right times.
>
> Imagine the full capability of this kind of "psychographic" advertising. In future Republican campaigns, a pro-gun voter whose Ocean score ranks him high on neuroticism could see storm clouds and a threat: The Democrat wants to take his guns away. A separate pro-gun voter deemed agreeable and introverted might see an ad

132 Rosenberg, Matthew, Confessore, Nicholas & Cadwalladr, Carole. "How Trump Consultants Exploited the Facebook Data of Millions." New York Times, 3/17/18.

emphasizing tradition and community values, a father and son hunting together."[133]

When this type of tactic is added to the fact that Facebook (and Twitter and YouTube among others) often carry and push fake news at all of us on a consistent basis, it argues for rigorous oversight of these media. Further, we all need to be taught that there is almost always a hidden agenda to these "news" stories, and that the default reaction should be to disbelieve, and perhaps report the story to an as-yet nonexistent authority.

The problem is not at all easy to solve, if we want to continue having even a minimal relationship with social media. The mere act of "liking" something, or following a group reveals something about who we are to prying eyes. Personally, I am into doo-wop music. I "like" songs posted and I am a member of several groups within that genre. This tells the alert observer that I am of a certain age, and so it is very possible that I will get "push" ads about retirement communities and cures for arthritis. It should be noted that this consequence of being on line is less odious than political targeting because at least the agenda of the message pusher is out in the open, while political targeting is intentionally covert.

---

133 Funk, McKenzie. "Cambridge Analytica and the Secret Agenda of a Facebook Quiz." New York Times, Op-Ed, 11/19/18.

As a child, I remember being repeatedly told, "Don't take candy from a stranger." Why? Because said stranger had an ulterior motive. Kidnapping and/or worse might ensue. While not quite as dire, "Don't believe anything that you hear on social media" might be a 21st century version of the candy parable. If the next generation can filter and perhaps discount any news from social media, the world will be a better place.

10) Given that the need to check our facts has increased in recent years, colleges and universities should develop a curriculum to support a new profession: that of a **Professional Fact Checker**. Among the courses in the curriculum might be:

1) Mathematics and estimation skills

2) Economics including consumerism of monetary goods, news and other information

3) Logic and critical thinking

4) Scientific method and thinking (not necessarily science).

5) Statistics and probability

6) The Law, forensic and debating skills

7) Psychology

8) Accounting, marketing and (truth in) advertising techniques

9) Research skills

The PFC would have to pass licensing requirements and, like judges, would be subject to peer review. Political ads would have to be vetted by them before they are aired. PFCs would be employed not only by fact checking organizations (<u>factcheck.org</u>, <u>politifact.org</u>), but by social media entities (Facebook, Twitter) to judge the acceptability of content. They would be one remedy to the onslaught of technology which puts more power in the hands of fewer and more extreme influencers. High school curricula would be designed to prepare students for majoring in PFC.

The profession of PFC is likely to be immediately coveted on many levels. If the curriculum was introduced in high school there would be competition to get into preparatory classes and eventually colleges which sponsored this major. This competition would ensure that bright, capable people competed for entry into this field. It would be esteemed as a profession, much as medicine, law and science are today. "After all, think of how you really persuade people. Do you do it by writing thoughtful essays that carefully marshal facts? That works some of the time. But the real way to persuade people is to create an attractive community that people want to join. If you do that, they'll bend their opinions to yours. If you want people to be reasonable, create groups where it's cool to be reasonable."[134] PFCs would be cool.

---

[134] Brooks, David. "The Art of Thinking Well." New York Times Op-Ed, 10/10/17.

Chapter 19: The Way Forward

If the reader recalls, this book started with a summary: *Confirmation bias, guided by deductive and inductive logic, driven by self-interest, catalyzed by technology, all within a person's unique echo chamber, leads to tribalism.*

First, the characteristics of echo chambers were described, and then discussed in relation to both exogenous events (Trump's ascent to the Presidency, income inequality, racial/religious differences) as well as endogenous processes (deductive/inductive logic, self-interest).

The last two chapters have suggested ways to reduce tribalism in echo chambers, both in general (by seeking facts, demanding ethical behavior, respecting expertise and developing analytical skills), and in the specific (teaching processes over facts, logic and logical fallacies, scientific method and statistics, ways of compromise, among others). It is also strongly felt that instilling these concepts/values/beliefs will take many years and must start as early in person's life as is possible.

There is one last point to be made, however. Are there clues to a general direction that humanity can take that will minimize the mistrust, fear and hatred that go along with increasing tribalism? To examine these clues, the concepts of acceptance and equality in relationships will be introduced. Here, acceptance in a relationship means that one will abide certain flaws in, or differences with, another person because the overall relationship is worth having or preserving. This kind of acceptance can be seen in lifelong friendships and long-lasting marriages.

The second concept is equality which, as used here, means that the two (or more) people who are interacting have (more or less) equal power. That is, one is not dominant and one submissive, or one is not a perpetrator and the other a victim. An example of equality might be found in a social organization or a large corporation, where all employees are more or less equal in stature, despite being of different races, religions, ethnicities or genders. It is believed that *there can be no acceptance without (relative) equality.*

We've previously discussed the many axes along which tribalism exists in America. Some of them are white vs. brown, religion vs. religion, Democrat vs. Republican, rich vs. poor, coast-dwellers vs. midwesterners, immigrants vs. natives, gay vs. straight. It is argued here that not all of these axes are equally important. In fact, there is *one axis that underpins most of the others, namely rich vs. poor, or income inequality.*

President Trump's attitude towards other nations may provide a good example. He is famously accused of using the adjective "s***hole" to refer to African countries, and of saying that Nigerians would not "go back to their huts," implying that the U.S. was preferable. And then he added a contrast by saying he'd prefer immigrants from Norway.[135] What did Trump imply when he used the terms "s***thole" and "their huts?" Yes, there are racial differences between Africans and Norwegians. But those terms he used also implies poverty. Trump assumed that Norwegians are fairly affluent, Africans impoverished.

"Things have been falling apart on multiple fronts since the 1970s: Political polarization has marched side by side with economic polarization, as income inequality has soared."[136] Income inequality is the basis for America-firsters not accepting immigrants; it is at the root of blue collar midwesterners resenting white collar coast intellectuals; and a major reason poor whites who resent their fate turn to a populist like Trump, who promises better times ahead. It is the basis of scapegoating; the Jews will take over the money system; the Mexicans will take our jobs. The poor subsist day to day and will forever resent, be jealous of, and perhaps even fear the power of the wealthy. Their echo chambers will seek out constructs supporting those resentments.

---

[135] Mortimer, Carolyn. "Norwegians tell Trump: We don't want to come to your s***hole country." Independent (U.K.), 1/12/18.

[136] Krugman, Paul. "What's the Matter With Trumpland?" New York Times Op-Ed. 4/2/18.

Can poor people ever feel comfortable around people with money? Or vice versa? Doubtful. If you are reading this, you are probably a "have." How many "have-not" friends are in your circle? As a generalization, people with money don't feel comfortable around poor people. Perhaps out of guilt, or out of the fear that they will take what you have. The echo chambers of those that have might contain rationalizations that those who are poor are lazy or milk the system. After all, you've earned and deserve every dollar you have, haven't you?

And poor people, again generalizing, may feel that the wealthy look down upon them, and may feel inadequate or jealous around those with money. Or even angry if they feel they've been screwed over by "the Man." Rich and poor don't mix well, and resentment is likely to be a part of the echo chambers of those less well off.

Inequality of power is also next to impossible to overcome. Can slaves ever accept slave owners? Can oppressed peoples accept their occupiers or conquerors? Can victims of sexual harassment or physical abuse ever accept their oppressors? Live with and resent, maybe. Accept, no. It's interesting however, that inequality of power diminishes drastically as income inequality disappears.

Consider people with roughly equal financial situations. Democrat can respect Republican, as long as it is reciprocal. Wealthy members of different religions have few problems with one another. We're equals, so you pray to whoever and wherever you want as long as I can do the same. Differences among people of different races are overcome in many situations, such as in the workplace, and in racially integrated neighborhoods and schools. Again, as long as incomes are relatively equal.

If we can agree that the *key to long-lasting and stable relationships is acceptance among equals*, this informs the way forward. Other things that divide us in our country and in our world diminish if, and as, incomes equalize. This argues that in America we have to reverse growing income inequality, through whatever means possible. Most economists agree that trickle-down policies don't work, but the Trump administration's trickle-down tax code may give us more data points. We should do whatever works.

Attempting to make income more equal across our states and regions has gotten caught up in the political wars. Some conservative states have turned down increased funding for Medicaid on principle and others have slashed taxes which was popular until their education systems suffered. "New Deal programs and public investment played a significant role in the great postwar convergence; conservative efforts to downsize government will hurt people all across America, but it will disproportionately hurt the very regions that put the G.O.P. in power."[137]

In terms of the greater world, globalization is much preferred to protectionism. Protectionism, in which each country puts its own needs first will favor wealthy countries. The same argument of "the rich get richer" applies to nations as well as people within nations.[138] The deck is stacked. Incidentally, most economists believe that globalization is better for the economies of all countries involved. They see free trade as a win-win, while protectionists see trade as a zero-sum game. Unfortunately, growing income inequality (and protectionist trade policies) are great news for fans of tribalism.

For these reasons and others, it is believed that income inequality is the central problem that humans will face in the twenty-first century.[139]

---

[137] ibid.

[138] This argument was made in Chapter 11.

[139] A strong argument can be made that income inequality underlies the threat posed by global climate change. Why? Who will be most affected by rising sea levels and more frequent natural disasters? Not the wealthy…

References

Adams, Taylor, Ma, Jessica & Thompson, Stuart A. "Trump Loves 'Fox & Friends.' Here's Why." New York Times, Opinion, 11/1/17.

Baraniuk, Chris. "Social media loves echo chambers, but the human brain helps create them." Quartz, 11/17/16. (https://qz.com/839982/social-media-loves-echo-chambers-but-the-human-brain-helps-create-them/)

Barnhorst, Amy. "The Mental Health System Can't Stop Mass Shooters." New York Times Op-Ed, 2/20/2018.

BBC News. "Donald Trump retweets far-right group's anti-Muslim videos." 11/29/17. http://www.bbc.com/news/world-us-canada-42166663

BBC News. "BBC to help students identify 'fake news'" 12/6/17. At: http://www.bbc.com/news/entertainment-arts-42242630

Blackwood, Kevin & Rubin, Max. "Improving Your Odds At Roulette." http://www.dummies.com/games/casino-games/improving-your-odds-at-roulette/

Blow, Charles. "Resistance, for the Win!" New York Times Op-Ed, 11/9/17.

Brennan Center for Justice. "Myth of Voter Fraud." New York University School of Law. At: https://www.brennancenter.org/issues/voter-fraud

Brooks, David. "The Art of Thinking Well." New York Times Op-Ed, 10/10/17.

Brooks, David. "When Politics Becomes Your Idol." New York Times Op-Ed, 10/30/17.

Brooks, David. "The Chaos After Trump." New York Times Op-Ed, 3/5/18.

Bruni, Frank. "Jesus' Parents and Roy Moore's Gall." New York Times Op-Ed, 11/10/17.

Cesca, Bob. "Debunking the Top 10 Most Egregious Republican Lies." Huffpost, The Blog, updated 5/24/14.

Coates, Ta-Nehisi. "The First White President." The Atlantic, October, 2017. https://www.theatlantic.com/magazine/archive/2017/10/the-first-white-president-ta-nehisi-coates/537909/

Blakeslee, Sarah. CRAAP test. Created at Meriam Library staff at California State University-Chico. Available at: https://www.csuchico.edu/lins/handouts/eval_websites.pdf

Dawkins, R. (2006). The Selfish Gene (30th Anniversary Edition). New York City: Oxford University Press.

Edsall, Thomas. "The Party of Lincoln Is Now the Party of Trump." New York Times Op-Ed, 10/26/17.

Edsall, Thomas B. "What Motivates Voters More Than Loyalty? Loathing." New York Times Op-Ed, 3/1/18.

Egan, Timothy. "The National Crackup." New York Times Op-Ed, 10/27/17.

Egan, Timothy. "The Vacuity of the Vice President." New York Times Op-Ed. 11/10/17.

Egan, Timothy. "We're With Stupid." New York Times Op-Ed, 11/17/17.

Egan, Timothy. "The Deserving Rich and the Deserving Poor." New York Times Op-Ed, 12/15/17.

Fiegerman, Seth. "Facebook's global fight against fake news." CNN Tech, 5/9/17. (http://money.cnn.com/2017/05/09/technology/facebook-fake-news/index.html)

Financial Samurai Blog. "What Percentage Of Americans Own Stocks Or Real Estate?" At: https://www.financialsamurai.com/what-percentage-of-americans-own-stocks-or-real-estate/

Fisher, Max & Keller, Josh. "What Explains U.S. Mass Shootings? International Comparisons Suggest an Answer." New York Times, The Interpreter, 11/7/17.

French, David. "Mueller's Investigation Won't Shake Trump's Base." New York Times, Op-Ed, 10/30/17.

Friedman, Tom. "Trump, Niger and Connecting the Dots." New York Times Op-Ed, 11/1/17.

Funk, McKenzie. "Cambridge Analytica and the Secret Agenda of a Facebook Quiz." New York Times, Op-Ed, 11/19/18.

Gallup News. "U.S. Stock Ownership Down Among All but Older, Higher-Income." 5/24/17.

Gardner, Howard. Frames of Mind: The Theory of Multiple Intelligences. Basic Books, 1983.

Gertz, Matthew. "I've Studied the Trump-Fox Feedback Loop for Months. It's Crazier Than You Think." politico.com, 1/5/18. At: https://www.politico.com/magazine/story/2018/01/05/trump-media-feedback-loop-216248

Ghose, Tia. ""Just a Theory": 7 Misused Science Words." Scientific American, 4/2/13.

Glover, Juleanna. "Are Republicans Ready to Join a Third Party?" New York Times Op-Ed, 1/29/18.

Goldberg, Michelle. "Tyranny of the Minority." New York Times Op-Ed, 9/25/17.

Goldberg, Michelle. "Anniversary of the Apocalypse." New York Times Op-Ed, 11/6/17.

Gribin, Anthony J. Selfonomics: How Broadly-Defined Self-Interest Explains Everything. 2014: ttgPress.

Hanson, Jim. Opinion. At http://www.foxnews.com/opinion/2018/01/28/no-russia-didnt-work-to-elect-trump-it-works-to-divide-americans-with-help-democrats.html

Heritage Foundation, The. At: http://thf-legal.s3.amazonaws.com/VoterFraudCases.pdf

Hess, Amanda. "How the Internet Fuels Paranoid Thinking." New York Times Video, 11/13/17.https://www.nytimes.com/video/arts/100000005417743/how-the-internet-fuels-paranoid-thinking.html

Internet Encyclopedia of Philosophy: a Peer-Reviewed Academic Resource. At: http://www.iep.utm.edu/ded-ind/

Investopedia. "The Generation Gap." At: http://www.investopedia.com/terms/g/generation-gap.asp

Jacoby, Susan. "Stop Apologizing for Being Elite." New York Times Op-Ed, 3/16/18.

Jarrett, Gregg. "Robert Mueller and his politically biased team of prosecutors need to go." Fox News, Politics, 12/9/17. At: http://www.foxnews.com/opinion/2017/12/08/gregg-jarrett-robert-mueller-and-his-politically-biased-team-prosecutors-need-to-go.html

Khan Academy. At: https://www.khanacademy.org/science/biology/intro-to-biology/science-of-biology/a/the-science-of-biology

Krugman, Paul. "The Centrist Cop-Out." New York Times Op-Ed, 7/28/11.

Krugman, Paul. "Republicans Against Science." New York Times Op-Ed, 8/28/11.

Krugman, Paul. "On Feeling Thankful but Fearful." New York Times Op-Ed, 11/23/17.

Krugman, Paul. "What's the Matter With Trumpland?" New York Times Op-Ed. 4/2/18.

mediabiasfactcheck. At: https://mediabiasfactcheck.com/2016/07/20/the-10-best-fact-checking-sites/

Meyer, Eugene L. "Stamped Out." New York Times Op-Ed, 9/29/17.

Mortimer, Carolyn. "Norwegians tell Trump: We don't want to come to your s***hole country." Independent (U.K.), 1/12/18.

notjustatheory.com. At: http://notjustatheory.com. Copyright 2007-2008.

Oehlheiser, Amy. "This is how Facebook's fake-news writers make money." Washington Post, 11/18/16.

Oge, Marge. "Looser Emissions Standards Will Hurt the Auto Industry." New York Times Op-Ed, 3/30/18.

Oliver, Vicki. 301 Smart Answers to Tough Business Etiquette Questions. 2015, Skyhorse Publishing Co.

Ortiz, Eric. "Apple's Tim Cook Says Dividing People a Greater Issue Than Russian Facebook Ads." NBC News, 11/1/17. https://www.nbcnews.com/tech/apple/apple-s-tim-cook-says-dividing-people-greater-issue-russian-n816536

Rice, Susan. "We Have Met the Enemy, and He Is Us." New York Times Op-Ed, 1/25/18.

Roberts, David. "America is facing an epistemic crisis." Vox, 11/2/17. At: https://www.vox.com/policy-and-politics/2017/11/2/16588964/america-epistemic-crisis

Ropeik, David. "How Tribalism Overrules Reason, and Makes Risky Times More Dangerous." BigThink, At: http://bigthink.com/risk-reason-and-reality/how-tribalism-overrules-reason-and-makes-risky-times-more-dangerous

Rosenberg, Matthew, Confessore, Nicholas & Cadwalladr, Carole. "How Trump Consultants Exploited the Facebook Data of Millions." New York Times, 3/17/18.

Schumaker, Erin. "How Republicans And Democrats Can Interpret Events SO Differently." Huffpost, updated 7/1/16.

Schumpeter, Joseph A. Capitalism, Socialism and Democracy. London: Routledge, 1942.

Seife, Charles. Proofiness: The Dark Arts of Mathematical Deception. 2010: Viking.

Setmayer, Tara. "Donald Trump and the Tyranny of the Minority." Daily Beast, 4/4/16.

Shapiro, Leslie. "Anatomy of a Russian Facebook ad." Washington Post, Business Analysis, 11/1/17.

Shribman, David M. "Yes, the Truth Still Matters." New York Times Op-Ed, 12/11/17.

Sitaraman, Ganesh. "Our Constitution Wasn't Built for This." New York Times Op-Ed, 9/16/17.

Solnit, Rebecca. "Tyranny of the Minority." Harper's Magazine, March, 2017.

Sullivan, Andrew. "America Wasn't Built for Humans." New York Magazine, 9/19/17.

Tackett, Michael & Wines, Michael. "Trump Disbands Commission on Voter Fraud." New York Times, Politics, 1/3/17.

Tumulty, Karen. "Two newspapers; two Benghazi headlines." Twitter Post, 6/29/16.

Vance, J.D. Hillbilly Elegy: A Memoir of a Family and Culture in Crisis. Harper Collins, 2016.

Vazquez, Maegan. "McCain again takes on Trump, says 'it's time to wake up'." CNN Politics, 10/31/17. At: http://www.cnn.com/2017/10/31/politics/john-mccain-naval-academy-speech/index.html

Waldman, Katy. "A Flight of Sycophancy: A line-by-line breakdown of Mike Pence's master class in toadyism." Slate, 12/21/17. At: http://www.slate.com/articles/news_and_politics/politics/2017/12/a_line_by_line_breakdown_of_mike_pence_s_master_class_in_toadyism.html

Wall Street Journal, "Senate Passes Revision of U.S. Tax Code." 12/2/17.

Wehner, Peter. "Seeing Trump Through a Glass, Darkly." New York Times Op-Ed, 10/7/17.

Yankah, Ekow N. "Can My Children Be Friends With White People?" New York Times, Sunday Review, 11/11/17.

"Your Logical Fallacy Is." At: https://yourlogicalfallacyis.com/strawman

Zeitz, Joshua. "Does the White Working Class Really Vote Against Its Own Interests?" Politico, 12/31/17. At: https://www.politico.com/magazine/story/2017/12/31/trump-white-working-class-history-216200?cid=apn

Zernike, Kate. "Christie Worried About Bridge Scandal, Report Finds." New York Times, 12/5/13.